Developing Literacy
WORD LEVEL

WORD-LEVEL ACTIVITIES FOR THE LITERACY HOUR

year

5

Ray Barker

Christine Moorcroft

A & C BLACK

Reprinted 1999 (3 times), 2001(twice), 2002, 2004, 2006
First published in 1998 by
A&C Black Publishers Limited
38 Soho Square, London W1D 3HB
www.acblack.com

ISBN-10: 0-7136-4967-4
ISBN-13: 978-0-7136-4967-3

The authors and publisher would like to thank the
following teachers for their advice in producing this
series of books: Tracy Adam; Ann Hart; Lydia Hunt; Hazel Jacob;
Madeleine Madden; Helen Mason; Yvonne Newman; Annette Norman;
Katrin Trigg; Judith Wells.

A CIP catalogue record for this book is
available from the British Library.

A & C Black uses paper produced with elemental chlorine-free pulp,
harvested from managed sustainable forests.

Printed in Great Britain by
St Edmundsbury Press Ltd, Bury St Edmunds, Suffolk.

Contents

Introduction

Developing Literacy: Word Level supports the teaching of reading and writing by providing a series of activities to develop essential skills in reading and spelling: word recognition and phonics. The activities are designed to be carried out in the time allocated to independent work during the Literacy Hour and therefore should be relatively 'teacher-free'. The focus is on children investigating words and spelling patterns, generating their own words in accordance with what they have learned and, if possible, recognising and devising rules and strategies to enable them to become independent in their recording and further investigation of language.

The activities presented in **Developing Literacy: Word Level** support the learning objectives of the National Literacy Strategy at word level. Each book
- includes activities which focus on phonics, spelling, word recognition and vocabulary;
- develops children's understanding of sound-spelling relationships;
- helps children to extend their vocabulary by challenging them to talk about and investigate the meanings of words which they find difficult;
- promotes independent work during the Literacy Hour;
- provides extension activities on each page which reinforce and develop what the children have learned;
- includes brief notes for teachers on most pages.

Some of the activities focus on the high/medium frequency words listed in the National Literacy Strategy's *Framework for Teaching*. These are lists of words which need to be recognised on sight. At Key Stage 1, they are words which the children need to know in order to tackle even very simple texts. Some are regular but others, such as 'said' and 'water', do not follow regular phonic spelling patterns. At Key Stage 2, there is an additional list of medium frequency words which children often have difficulty in spelling.

The activities are presented in a way which requires the children to read the words rather than just guessing the answers or 'filling in the spaces'. Sometimes they are asked to turn over the sheet and then write a list of words or a partner could read the words aloud for them to write. Working with partners or in groups is encouraged so that the children can check one another's reading and co-operate to complete the activities or play games. It is also useful for the children to show their work to the rest of the class and to explain their answers during the plenary session in order to reinforce and develop their own learning and that of others in the class.

Children need to 'Look, Say, Cover, Write and Check' (LSCWCh) words on a regular basis in order to learn their spellings. This has been indicated by the following logo:  It is essential that children learn the habit of looking up and checking words in a dictionary. This has been indicated by the following logo:

Use a dictionary.

Extension

Each activity sheet ends with a challenge (**Now try this!**) which reinforces and extends the children's learning and provides the teacher with an opportunity for assessment. Where children are asked to carry out an activity, the instructions are designed to enable them to work independently, for example
- Write **six** other words with **dge** or **ge**.

The teacher may decide to amend this before photocopying, depending on his or her knowledge of the children's abilities and speed of working.

- **List six other words which come from other countries.**
- **Write the six words in sentences.**

Organisation

For many of the activities it will be useful to have a range of dictionaries, thesauruses, fiction and non-fiction books, coloured pencils, counters, scissors and squared paper available and easily accessible. Several activities can be re-used to provide more practice in different letters or sounds, by masking the words and/or letters and replacing them with others of the teacher's choice, such as on page 18.

To help teachers to select appropriate learning experiences for their pupils, the activities are grouped into sections within each book. The pages are **not** intended to be presented in the order in which they appear in the books.

The teacher should select the appropriate pages to support the work in progress. Some children may be weak in areas which were covered in previous years. If so, teachers can refer to the **Developing Literacy: Word Level** book for the previous year for appropriate activities, which may be adapted. For more able children the teacher may want to adapt the activity sheets by masking the words and letters and replacing them with more demanding examples.

Many activities will be completed entirely on the activity sheets. On others, particularly in the extension activities, the children will need to work either on the back of the page, on a separate sheet of paper or in an exercise book.

It is useful for children to keep their own word banks containing the new words they have learned. These could be general or for a specific topic on which the class is working. Children should be encouraged to make a note of any words they find difficult so that they can add them to the word bank. The class could also have a word wall display to which they can add new words.

Structure of the Literacy Hour

The recommended structure of the Literacy Hour for Key Stage 2 is as follows:

Whole class introduction	15 min	Shared text work (balance of reading and writing) in which the teacher reads or writes a piece of text with the class, to elicit participation in discussion of the topic to be taught.
Whole class activity	15 min	Focused word work or sentence work in which the children contribute to a teacher-led activity arising from the whole class introduction.
Group work Independent work (rest of class)	20 min	The teacher works with groups of children on guided text work. The other children could work independently, for example, from an activity in one of the **Developing Literacy** series (**Word Level**, **Sentence Level** or **Text Level**).
Whole class plenary session	10 min	The teacher leads a review of what has been learned by consolidating teaching points, reviewing, reflecting and sharing the children's ideas and the results of their work.

The following flow chart shows an example of the way in which an activity from this book can be used to achieve the required organisation of the Literacy Hour.

Doubling the final consonant (page 31)

Whole class introduction	15 min

Use a shared text which contains such words as hum, stop, hop, top, slap. Ask the children comprehension questions to elicit the words as answers. Rhyming by analogy will enable them to list others, such as mop, tap. Ask further questions to elicit a change of word ending, for example, 'What are the children doing?' - 'They are skipping, running, hopping'; 'What do we call someone who runs?' - 'A runner'; 'What have the children just done?' - 'They have hopped'. What do they notice about the spelling of the words?

Whole class activity	15 min

Concentrate on the board containing the two lists of words. The children can highlight the root word by underlining and can then list the range of suffixes: **ed, ing, er**. Guide them to notice the doubling of final consonants when word-building. Generate other examples and list those which do not work, such as come and hope (compare with hop). Raise the question: when do we double the final consonant?

Independent work	20 min

The activity sheet is used to involve children in the investigation. Using dictionaries, they make as many words as possible using the suffixes and then answer the questions to write their rule. They should notice that the words are single syllabled. When the final consonant doubles it is preceded by a vowel, for example, hop (hopped). Grammatical considerations should also be considered: are there such words as swimmed, readed or runned?

Group work	20 min

The teacher works with at least one group on guided text work.

Whole class plenary session	10 min

Children from the various groups tell the rest of the class what they have noticed and learned about doubling the final consonant, writing new words on the word wall. The teacher monitors the learning and assesses the children to ensure that work for the next Literacy Hour is appropriate and meaningful. Finally, the rule should be written out and displayed for future use.

Teachers' notes

Very brief notes are provided at the end of most pages. They give ideas for maximising the effectiveness of the activity sheets. They may make suggestions for the whole-class introduction, the plenary session or, possibly, follow up work using an adapted version of the activity sheet. Before photocopying, these notes could be masked.

Teachers' note French and Latin have had considerable influence on English. Make lists of other French and Latin words the children can find. Discuss how French pronunciation has changed the spelling of words, for example, garage, ballet.

**Developing Literacy
Word Level Year 5
© A & C Black 1998**

Using the activity sheets

Brief information is given here about the work within each section of **Developing Literacy: Word Level Year 5.** Suggestions are also given for additional activities.

Spelling strategies

The focus of the work in Years 5 and 6 builds upon the phonic work of early years, but is more concerned with the children formulating rules which will help them to become independent spellers. Therefore, activities in this section ask them to investigate spelling, play with words, generate new ones according to rules and record what they find difficult. Children need to be able to work independently during the Literacy Hour, or the management issues for the teacher, working closely with a group at all times will make high-quality interaction difficult.

Stepping Stones (page 9) and **Rhyme quiz** (page 10) build upon earlier phonic and rhyming work. They require the children to listen to words and to change various sounds. The focus is on fun and this kind of exercise will prove invaluable to teachers in the plenary session at the end of the Literacy Hour when the children can present to others what they have found and even test them. You can monitor the learning and assess if extra work needs to be given. Children with learning difficulties could join with other children and thus still be part of a successful team.

Can you speak 'End'? (page 11) and **Letter strings** (page 12) build upon the idea of children being able to identify and copy patterns in words. Giving children codes and asking them to write words using codes is a good way to allow them to break down words into constituent parts and see how the words are put together. This sheet asks the children to concentrate particularly on vowel **sounds** - not just vowels. They will have to ensure that they know where the vowels are and insert the 'end' appropriately. Much fun can be had by trying to speak this special language and this can be easily linked with phonics, for example, what happens when **e** and **a** come together, as in bead, bread, bear? How are they pronounced? **Secret code** (page 59) in the final section can also be used for this purpose. There are many common patterns in words (not necessarily letter strings), recognition of which can assist in building up words. **Letter strings** (page 12) concentrates on three patterns: **our, ture** and **ssion**. These all contain phonemes which can be pronounced in a different way, so recognition within words is essential. The class could keep a running record of such words on the class word wall and these can be used during a guided or group writing session. Thus the activity sheets can also be seen as a starting point for further investigation.

Children can also learn a great deal about the structure and meaning of words by looking at beginnings and endings. The words 'prefix' and 'suffix' should have already been used and the metalanguage should become a part of the children's vocabulary. In **Using beginnings** (page 13), **The suffix machine** (page 14) and **Investigating ion** (page 15), the aim is for children to investigate words they have generated and see if they can discover a rule or a principle which will make their spelling more accurate in the future for example, if they know that 'extra' means 'more', they may able to spell 'extraordinary' more accurately. When building lists of words, it is essential that the teacher and the children interrogate (investigate) them, for example, circle common letters or phonemes, underline the letters before and after. Are they always vowels? Are the vowels long or short? What about the consonants? Are they hard or soft? In many cases, adding prefixes or suffixes does not change the spelling of the root word at all, and if the children can come to realise this they will learn to spell much more complicated words, such as 'disappear' or 'thankful'. Again, the plenary session is the time for the teacher to make the most of the words which children have generated and to tease out any ideas which will help them. The Venn diagram in **Investigating ion** (page 15) is a good way to analyse patterns. You should model this principle with children at first, asking them for suggestions as to which words could be written in certain sections. At first, they may find it difficult that some words may fit into more than one category. Blanking out some of the Venn diagram, as on the sheet, will help.

Qu (page 16), **Wedges** (page 17) and **Letter string acrobats** (page 18) concentrate on specific letter patterns, for example, **q** is always followed by **u**. The reason for doing this is that the children can use the patterns to build new words and to recognise the patterns within the words. Often this is difficult for them to understand until they have experimented with words themselves. The children should be hypothesising as to why some sounds are soft and others are hard. Could it be that **g** followed by **e** is always soft? Are there any more examples to prove this?

Breaking words into syllables is always a helpful spelling strategy. In **Syllable magnets** (page 19) the words need to be analysed to see what changes have taken place. Throughout this book, the children are strongly encouraged to use dictionaries to check their spelling themselves before asking the teacher. Another useful technique, which leads on to work using etymological dictionaries, is to use known words within words. **Using parts of words** (page 20) encourages children to generate difficult words, whose meanings they will have to look up. The work here also reflects prefix and suffix work, as the parts of the words come from ancient Greek or Latin.

Homophones have been dealt with in previous years. **Sniff out that homophone** (page 21) revises them and leads into more difficult work on **Homographs** (page 22). It is also useful to develop the idea of mnemonics as a strategy for remembering difficult spellings, as in **Remembering spellings** (page 24). Children's ideas could be made into wall displays so that they can be consulted whenever the issues arise. If the mnemonics are visual the children are more likely to remember: for example, temperature - hot temper, could provide a good opportunity for cartoons, as could elephant - ant.

Spelling conventions and rules

Much of the spelling work of Years 5 and 6 builds upon and revises the work of previous years. **Plurals rule chart** (page 25) provides a useful record sheet which the children could keep. It could also be made into a large wall version, which could be completed with the whole class in a shared writing session and then kept for reference. The examples could be provided from the shared reading text.

In **Negative prefixes** (page 26) and **Prefix opposites** (page 27), the children look at the meaning of prefixes and the fact that some prefixes have opposites. Children are rarely aware of the fact that negative prefixes do not change the spelling of the root word, so it is essential to reinforce the concept of root words and how these can be extended. The visual idea in **Extending words** (page 28) is that root words are solid like houses and these can have extensions built on to them, before and after. It should be noted that many of these sheets are investigatory and that they do not necessarily have 'correct answers'. The children might list completely different words. The teacher can discuss any issues during the plenary session. The other image used in **Root words fireworks** (page 29) is that of words exploding that is, they are fragments which come together to make words. This could be used as a display idea with the children adding their words to the fireworks on the wall as they come across them in their own reading or writing.

Much of this section, such as **full and all words** (page 30), requires the children to look carefully at words and to find or propose rules. They need to look at changes of spelling when word-building. Checking in a dictionary is essential for these activities. Many activities can be dealt with in pairs and games can be played quietly and results recorded. Investigation should focus on the words created, for example in **Doubling the final consonant** (page 31). The nature of English is that most rules have exceptions, which children should be aware of. However, there are far fewer exceptions to learn than words which regularly apply to a rule! **Silent e** (page 37) demonstrates that the vowel should change from a short vowel (h**a**t) to a long vowel (h**a**te) when e is added, whereas unstressed vowels in polysyllabic words follow no particular rule. The ability to split words into syllables, and to build syllables to make words, is a useful spelling strategy practised in **Long word spelling** (page 36).

Difficult words have been included because children like to read and learn long words; it gives them a real sense of achievement. Such words have only been incorporated when the words follow the rules or principles exemplified, such as 'annually' in **ly** (page 38) and 'financially' in **Lovely words** (page 39). In **i before e** (page 40) the children should be identifying the patterns in the words, that is, circling the **c** and checking that the word rhymes with 'me'.

Much of the work at Year 5 at word-level links with sentence-level activities. Knowledge of parts of speech is essential and the use of appropriate language, such as adverb and pronoun, should be encouraged. The changes in spelling which occur when words change from one part of speech to another, for example, from an adjective to a noun, as in **Transforming words** (page 42), should be developed during shared reading sessions by the use of questioning, for example, 'It says that the princess is beautiful. The word describes the princess. What part of speech is this? Suppose we want to talk about the quality she has? What would this be?' **Words ending in y** (page 41) and **New word endings** (page 43) give children a chance to see that words can be transformed, but also encourages them to develop concepts of word roots and appropriate language in their writing and grammar.

Vocabulary extension

This work builds upon, and reinforces, the word work of previous years, for example, in continuing the use of rhyme and analogy and in helping the children to devise simple strategies for learning spelling. It also uses the high/medium frequency words from the *Framework for Teaching* and words from other curriculum areas to provide simple games and puzzles which may provide an easier way of sending words home.

Work in Year 5 is focused on extended writing activities and on providing appropriate language to help the children to do this, as in **Synonyms for describing faces** (page 44), **Antonym 'Snap'** (page 45), **Similes** (page 47), **Using metaphors** (page 48), **Animal onomatopoeia** and **Sound poems** (pages 49-50). The children should be given the opportunity to discover that language is not always literal and that it is possible to have fun with words and to create images in many startling ways. The sheets are seen as ways of introducing the ideas and practising them, but the language principles should be developed in extended writing tasks in the shared and guided writing sessions and at other times other than the Literacy Hour.

Language derivation is dealt with, working from the premise that English is not a static language but is changing and developing all the time. **Computer words** (page 55) is particularly pertinent here as new words are coming into our language every day in this area. **Foreign phrases** (page 51) and **World English** (page 52) help the children to recognise that many words and phrases come from foreign languages which makes them difficult to spell. **American accents and words** (page 53) and **A cockney poem** (page 54) could result in a discussion of standard English. Teachers could also use these as shared texts to make a point about different accents as well as about dialect words. The children will be using many American words from films and television without knowing it, for example 'lieutenant'.

The section ends with fun activities designed to challenge the children to think of words and letters as things which can be changed and it gives them the power to do this. The words provided are often from other curriculum areas, as in **Maths words** (page 56). **'A lot of' words** (page 57) and **'Get' new words** (page 58) concentrate on over-used words and the need to vary vocabulary according to descriptive context. Much of this work will arise from shared text work at the beginning of the Literacy Hour, identifying appropriate use of vocabulary. It can be developed in shared and guided writing, especially in poetry. Again, the children could record interesting and new words on the class word wall, which will give the class teacher a chance to monitor language development and provide a bank of useful words from which to develop writing activities. New words identified should be challenging, not those readily available to children. Use computers where possible to change and edit work more easily. Many computers have their own word bank facility and a thesaurus.

The following pages provide practice in using alphabetical order and important reference sources: **Secret Code** (page 59), **Which dictionary quartile?** (page 60), **Alphabetical order** (page 61), **Meanings game** and **Blank meanings cards** (pages 62 and 63) and **My own dictionary** (page 64). The most important thing is that the children become more independent in their investigation of spelling words. The teacher should have a range of dictionaries available, some easy and some adult-focused.

Answers
Pages for which answers have been provided have been marked in the Teachers' notes with an asterisk (*).

Stepping stones (page 9): other answers may be possible.
car, bar, bat, but, bus
cold, cord, card, ward, warm
hard, card, cart, part, port, sort, soft
ride, tide, time, tame, tale, talk, walk

Qu (page 16):
queen, quiet, quilt, quarter, queue, quartet, quick, quiz, quarrel
Across: 3. aquarium, 4. antique, 6. unique, 7. frequent
Down: 1. mosquito, 2. squirrel, 4. aqueduct, 5. marquee

World English (page 52):
India: shampoo, curry, pyjamas (or Persian).
Italy: studio, pizza, spaghetti, piano, opera, umbrella.
French: garage, traffic, café.
Persian: caravan, bazaar, pyjamas (or Indian).
Norwegian : ski. Mexican/Aztec: chocolate. African: cola.
Finnish: sauna. Greek: gymnasium.
Old English: pepper. South American: barbecue.

American accents and words (page 53):
trunk - car boot, hood - car bonnet, elevator - lift, ice box - fridge, apartment - a flat, subway - the underground railway, sidewalk - pavement, gas - petrol

Computer words (page 55):
monitor, keyboard, printer, CD ROM, hard drive, modem, floppy disk, mouse

A lot of words (page 57):
ships - fleet
cattle - herd
snow - blizzard
money - fortune
applause - ovation
new houses - estate
passages - labyrinth
people who want to cause trouble - mob
people who want to worship - congregation

'Get' new words (page 58):
Across: 3. mount, 5. diminish, 6. improve, 7. recover, 10. prosper
Down: 1. melt, 2. begin, 4. obstruct, 8. embark, 9. grow

Glossary of terms used

analogy Recognising a word, phoneme or pattern in known words and applying this to new, unfamiliar words.
antonym A word with a meaning opposite to another, for example, hot - cold.
etymological dictionary A specialist dictionary which deals with the derivation of words.
homonyms Words which are spelled the same, have the same pronunciation, but a different meaning, for example, **Wave** good-bye to your cousin. Watch out for the tidal **wave**!
homographs Words which are spelled the same, pronounced differently and mean something different, for example, **bow, wind**.
homophones Words which sound the same, mean something different and are spelled differently, for example, **poor, paw, pour**
onset The initial consonant or consonant cluster of a word or syllable, for example, **tr**ain, **scr**ape, **sk**ate.
letter string A string of letters which remains constant in spelling, for example, **ight**
metalanguage The language we use when talking about language.
metaphor Writing about something as if it were something else, for example, education is the key to your future.
mnemonics Systems devised to aid memory, for example, I'll be your fri**END** to the **END**
phoneme The smallest unit of sound in a word. A phoneme can be represented by one to four letters, for example, st**ay**, s**igh**t.
phonics The relationship between sounds and the written form of a language.
rhyme The use of words which have the same sound in their final syllable, for example, **fox/rocks**, **sore/door**.
rime The part of a word or syllable which contains the vowel and final consonant or consonant cluster, for example, sh**eep**, sl**ow**, f**oal**.
syllable A rhythmic segment of a word, for example, can (1 syllable) , can- op- y (3 syllables), tel- e- vis- ion (4 syllables).

Stepping stones

- Change one letter at a time to make a new word.
- Underline the letter you have changed.
- Your 'start' and 'end' words are given to you.

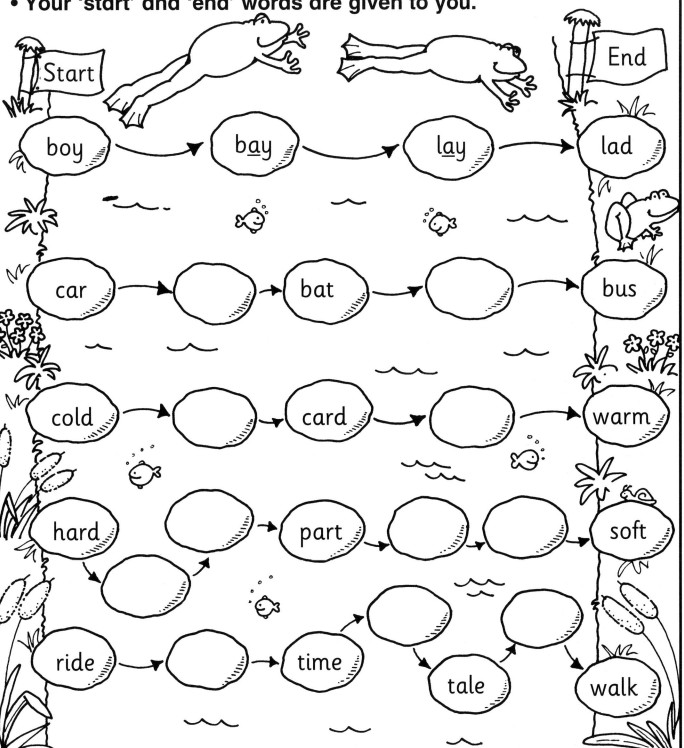

Start | boy → b<u>a</u>y → lay → lad | End

car → ⬡ → bat → ⬡ → bus

cold → ⬡ → card → ⬡ → warm

hard → ⬡ → part → ⬡ → ⬡ → soft

ride → ⬡ → time → ⬡ → tale → ⬡ → walk

Now try this!

- **Work out four lines of stepping stones with new words.**
- **Give them to a partner to solve with only the 'start' and 'end' words.**

Teachers' note* All children should be able to complete at least a few of these. The earlier examples concentrate on cvc words to ensure that all the children can report their findings during the plenary session.

Developing Literacy
Word Level Year 5
© A & C Black

- **Read the clues. Write the rhyming words.**
- **Circle the parts of the words which rhyme.**

plump kitten

f(a t)

c(a t)

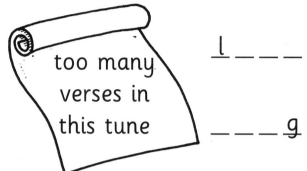

heat the grease

b _ _ _

_ _ _ l

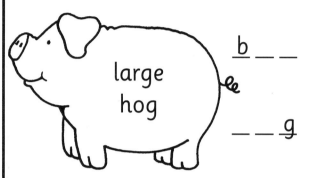

large hog

b _ _

_ _ g

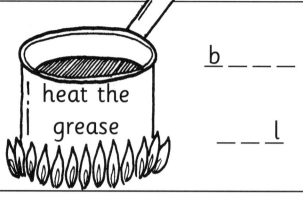

too many verses in this tune

l _ _ _

_ _ _ g

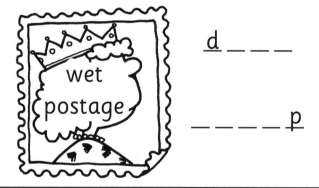

wet postage

d _ _ _

_ _ _ _ p

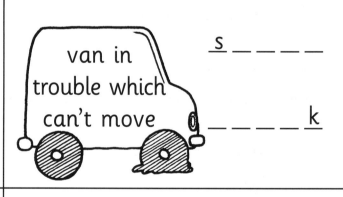

van in trouble which can't move

s _ _ _ _ _

_ _ _ _ k

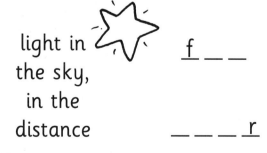

light in the sky, in the distance

f _ _

_ _ _ r

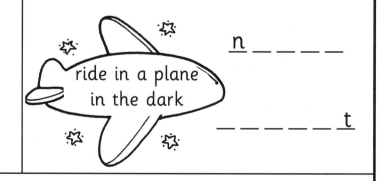

ride in a plane in the dark

n _ _ _ _

_ _ _ _ _ t

Now try this!

- **Work with a partner. Make up other rhymes.**
- **Draw and write clues for them. Test them on a friend.**

Teachers' note This is a fun way to develop and revise earlier work on rhyming by analogy. It is a useful way for the children to remember how to spell certain sounds, for example, the **a** is the **a** in fat cat, not the **a** in space race, using the letter **e** to make the vowel long.

Developing Literacy
Word Level Year 5
© A & C Black

Can you speak 'End'?

- **Someone has invented a new language. Before every vowel she writes** `end` **. So the word 'today' is spelled** t `end` **od** `end` **a** `end` **y.**

@ e i o u y

- **Have fun reading the words aloud.**

- **Write the English word which is being spelled in 'End' language.**

bendallendoendon _____

mendothender _____

grendeendat _____

thendosende _____

endapplende _____

- **Write your full name in 'End' language.**

_____

- **Spell these words in 'End' language.**

important _____

different _____

swimming _____

sometimes _____

children _____

across _____

something _____

Now try this!

- **Write a message in 'End' for a partner to solve.**

Teachers' note The children will be focusing on the vowels as they need to find their position to insert the code. This is a useful device to focus their attention on particular parts of words, for example, syllables or letter strings.

Developing Literacy
Word Level Year 5
© A & C Black

Letter strings

Each word contains one of three letter strings.

- Read the words aloud. Circle the letter strings.
- Write each letter string at the top of one of the notepads.
- Write each word on one of the notepads.

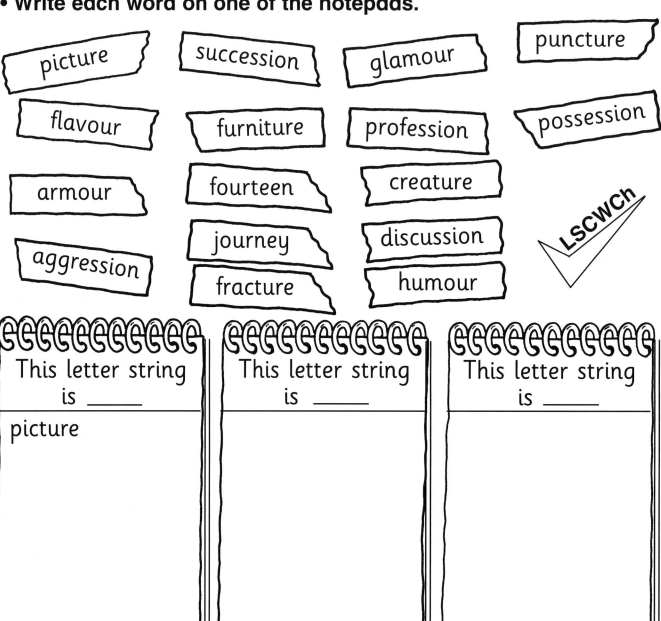

picture   succession   glamour   puncture

flavour   furniture   profession   possession

armour   fourteen   creature

aggression   journey   discussion

fracture   humour

LSCWCh

This letter string is _____

picture

This letter string is _____

This letter string is _____

Now try this!

- **Write eight of the words in sentences to show their meanings.**
- **Think of a letter string and list five words which contain the string.**

Teachers' note The idea is to isolate words so that the children can investigate spelling patterns. Often they cannot do this in their own written work through editing and redrafting because they are too concerned with content or presentation. Use the same idea with other letter strings.

Developing Literacy
Word Level Year 5
© A & C Black

Using beginnings

- **Add prefixes to the root words to make new words.**

Prefixes

dis	micro
extra	photo
sub	aqua
anti	super

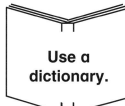

Use a dictionary.

Root words

approve	ordinary	appear
body	terrestrial	way
human	scope	graph
wave	copy	lung
social	marine	market

New words

disapprove _____ _____ _____

_____ _____ _____ _____

_____ _____ _____ _____

_____ _____ _____ _____

- **Does the spelling of the root word change? _____**
- **Complete the chart showing what you have discovered about the meaning of these prefixes.**

Prefix	Meaning		Prefix	Meaning

Now try this!

- **Write eight of the new words in sentences to show their meanings.**
- **Think of two other prefixes and make eight new words.**

LSCWCh

Teachers' note Many of the words here are difficult because they are from Greek or Latin, but the children are given limited options so they are in control of the word-building. Emphasise the final rule – the root word does not change. This should help the children to spell 'disappear' and 'disappoint' correctly!

Developing Literacy Word Level Year 5 © A & C Black

The suffix machine

- **Look at the suffix in each wheel.**
- **Think of words which end with this suffix. Write them on the wheel.**

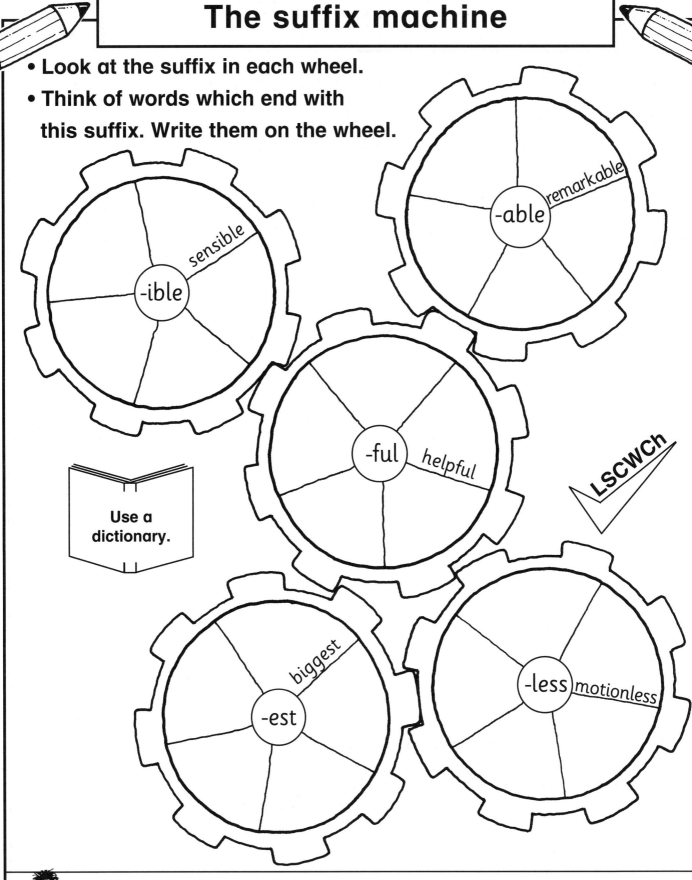

-ible · sensible

-able · remarkable

-ful · helpful

Use a dictionary.

LSCWCh

-est · biggest

-less · motionless

Now try this!

- **List any changes made to the spelling of the root word when you add the suffix, for example,** *sense* + *ible* = **sensible.**
- **Write a rule. Write four other examples to prove your rule.**

Teachers' note Lead the children, through further brainstorming and listing of words, to the understanding that **able** is generally added to complete words and **ible** to incomplete words.

**Developing Literacy
Word Level Year 5
© A & C Black**

Investigating ion

Adding ion to the end of a word is not always easy. You may have to add or take off some letters.

- Add ion to these words. Complete the chart.

create

perfect

inspect

subtract

opposite

protect

compete

Use a dictionary.

LSCWCh

add

dictate

Word	Word with ion
compete	competition

Word	Word with ion

- Write the ion words on to the Venn diagram.

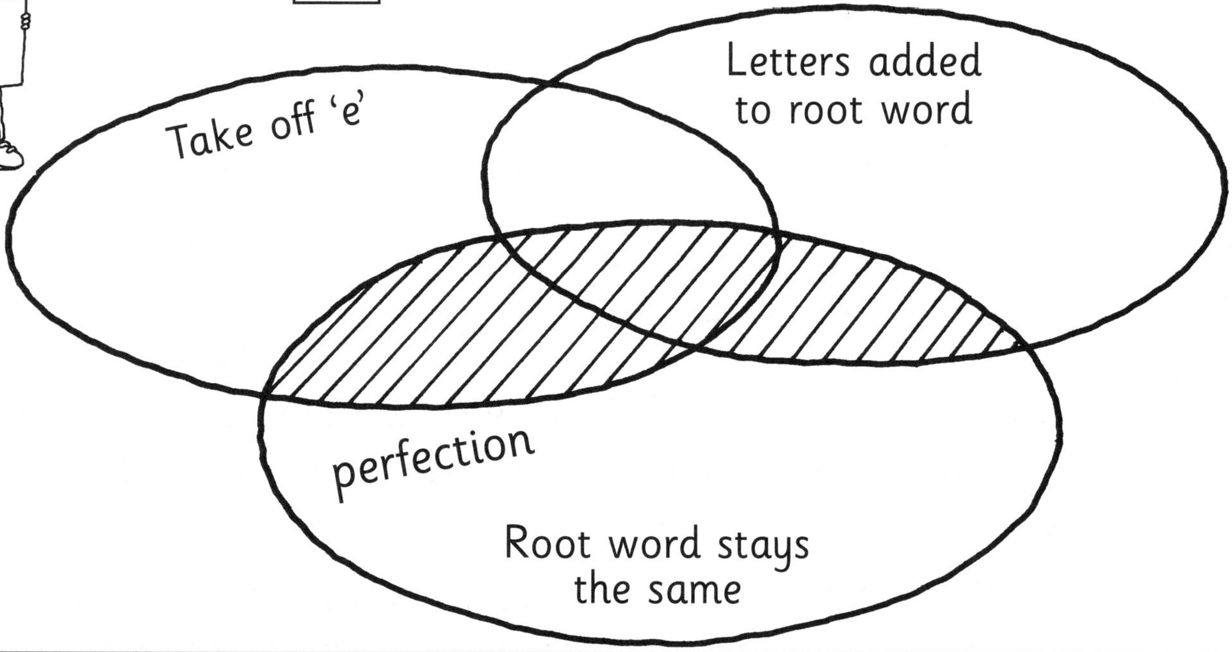

Now try this!

Take off 'e'

Letters added to root word

perfection

Root word stays the same

Teachers' note The Venn diagram concept is a useful one for shared word-level work because the children can add words to the diagram at the front of the class.

Developing Literacy
Word Level Year 5
© A & C Black

q is always followed by u .

• **Read the clues. Write the answers.**

q	u	a c k
q	u	_ _ _ _
q	u	_ _ _ _ _
q	u	_ _ _ _ _
q	u	_ _ _ _ _ _
q	u	_ _ _ _
q	u	_ _ _ _ _ _
q	u	_ _ _ _
q	u	_ _
q	u	_ _ _ _ _ _

a game of questions

not noisy

noise made ✓ by ducks

King's wife

cover for bed

one of four equal parts

a line of people waiting

speedy

four musicians

an argument

• **qu is in the middle of these words.**
Complete the puzzle.

LSCWCh

Clues across

3. Tank for fish (8).

4. Something old (7).

6. Only one of its kind (6).

7. Happening often (8).

Use a dictionary.

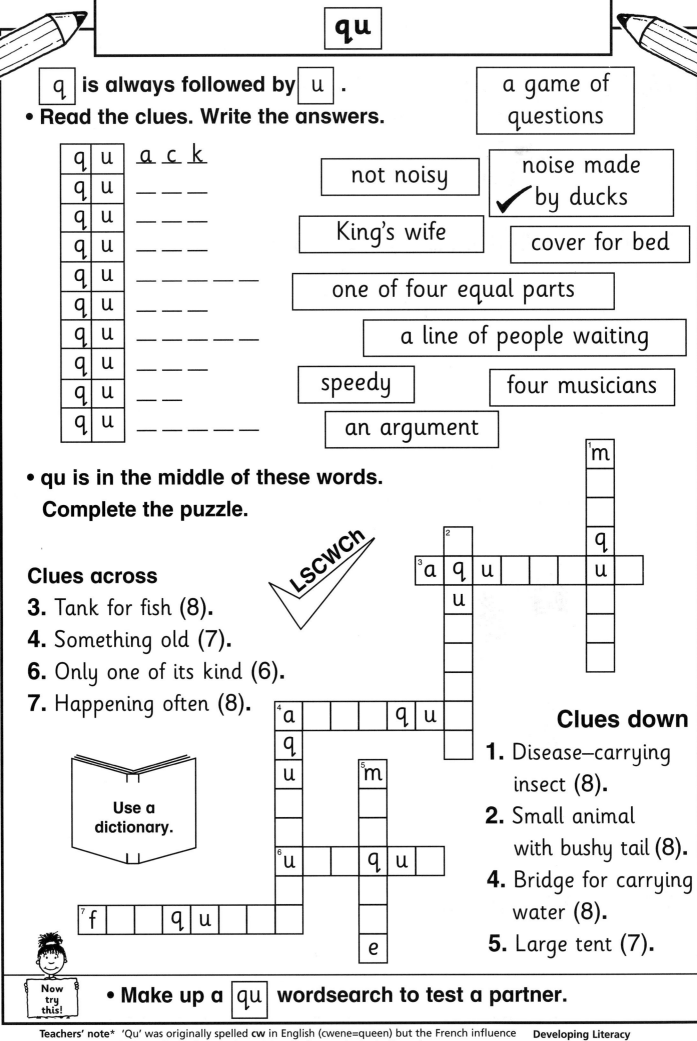

Clues down

1. Disease–carrying insect (8).

2. Small animal with bushy tail (8).

4. Bridge for carrying water (8).

5. Large tent (7).

Now try this!

• **Make up a** qu **wordsearch to test a partner.**

Teachers' note* 'Qu' was originally spelled **cw** in English (cwene=queen) but the French influence changed it. Teach the spelling of queue by reciting the letters rhythmically, as in a song. Exceptions to the rule are 'coq au vin' and Qatar (from other languages).

Developing Literacy
Word Level Year 5
© A & C Black

- All these words have the sound `dge` .

- Join the wedges to make the words. Write the word.

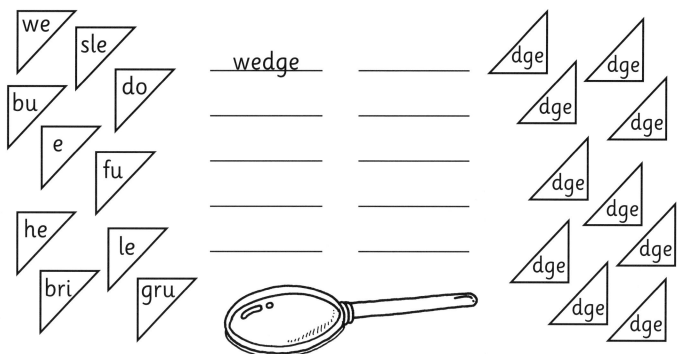

we	sle		wedge	_____	dge	dge
bu	do		_____	_____	dge	dge
e	fu		_____	_____	dge	dge
he	le		_____	_____	dge	dge
bri	gru		_____		dge	dge

- Investigate the words by answering these questions.

★ Where does `dge` come in all these words?

★ What comes before the `dge` ?

★ Is the vowel sound short or long?

- What have you found out about `dge` words?

- Explain how these words are different from the ones above.

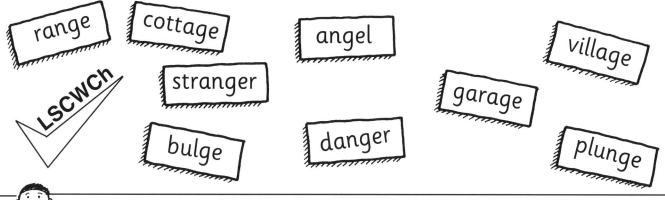

range   cottage   angel   village

LSCWCh

stranger   garage

bulge   danger   plunge

Now try this!

- Write six other words with `dge` or `ge` .
- Use them in sentences to show what they mean.

Teachers' note ge is a common letter string. The children should be able to develop rules to help them in their independent strategies, for example, dge at the end of words has a short vowel before it.

Developing Literacy
Word Level Year 5
© A & C Black

Letter string acrobats

- **Build acrobat pyramids using each letter string as a starting point.**

You need not use all the squares.

i	n		
r	i	n	g
s	t	i	n	g
s	i	n	g	l	e
s	i	n	g	i	n	g

b	a	n	g

a	n	g

i	t	t

l	i	t	t	l	e

a	g	e

e	a

Now try this!

- **Make sure you know the meanings of the words.**
- **Use** `air`, `amp`, `aid` **and** `all` **to make other acrobat pyramids.**

18

Teachers' note Because some of the word-building from the letter strings is quite challenging, begin by giving the children individual examples to complete and share with the class before they tackle this page. They can try to write long words but do not have to fill all the squares.

Developing Literacy
Word Level Year 5
© A & C Black

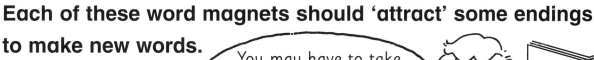

Syllable magnets

Each of these word magnets should 'attract' some endings to make new words.

You may have to take some letters away before adding the ending.

Use a dictionary.

- Write as many new words as you can.
- Divide the syllables with a line. Write the number of syllables in brackets.

Endings

write   writ/ing (2) _____

with   _____

where   _____

walk   _____

under   _____

sudden   _____

follow   _____

treat   _____

open   _____

every   _____

happy   _____

friend   _____

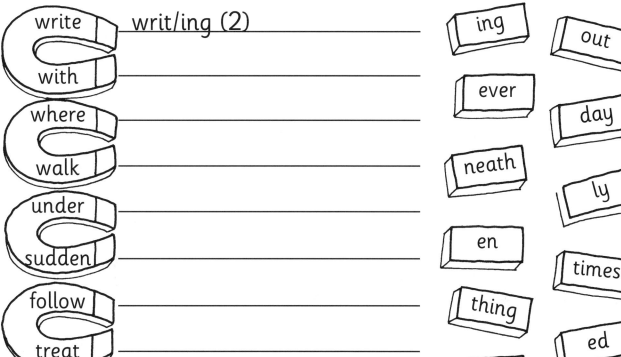

ing   out   ever   day   neath   ly   en   times   thing   ed   ment   ness   er   ship   where

LSCWCh

Now try this!

- Write five other words to which you can add some of the endings above.
- List the new words you can make.
- Circle all the words in which the root word changed when the ending was added. Write a rule.

Teachers' note In this activity, it is worth noting the dropping of the final **e** and the change from **y** to **i** in **happiness**, but generally the root remains unchanged.

Developing Literacy
Word Level Year 5
© A & C Black

Using parts of words

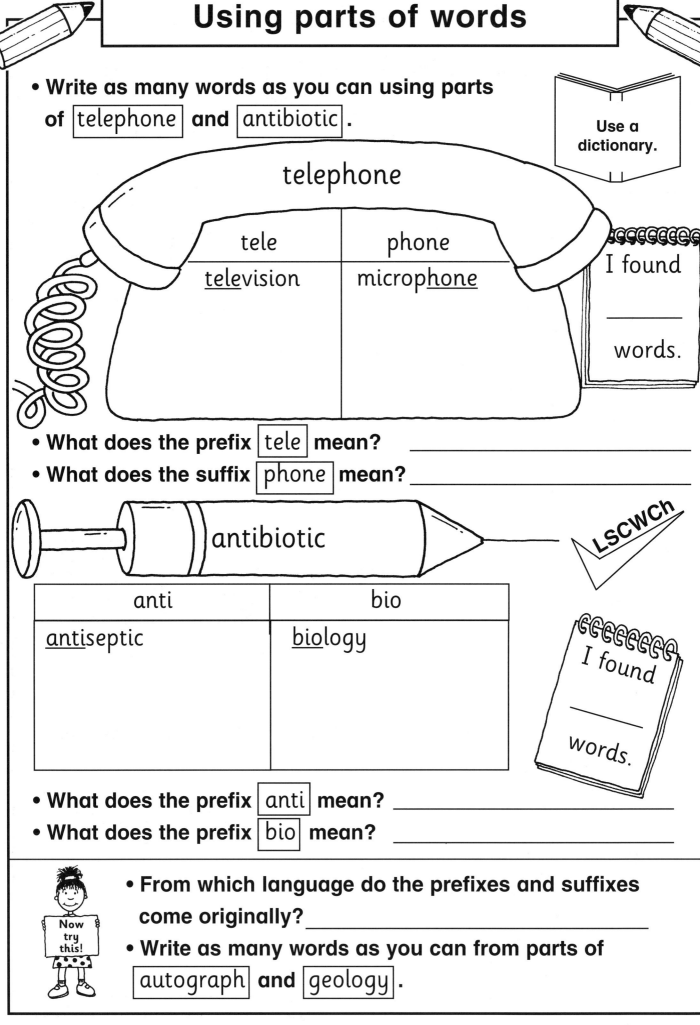

- **Write as many words as you can using parts of** `telephone` **and** `antibiotic`.

Use a dictionary.

telephone

tele	phone
tele̲vision	micro<u>phone</u>

I found _____ words.

- **What does the prefix** `tele` **mean?** _____
- **What does the suffix** `phone` **mean?** _____

antibiotic

LSCWCh

anti	bio
<u>anti</u>septic	<u>bio</u>logy

I found _____ words.

- **What does the prefix** `anti` **mean?** _____
- **What does the prefix** `bio` **mean?** _____

Now try this!

- **From which language do the prefixes and suffixes come originally?** _____
- **Write as many words as you can from parts of** `autograph` **and** `geology`.

Teachers' note The children should be able to find a large number of words, as the parts of the words are common technical terms. Generate more words from the parts of the words, for example, other words which contain **micro** or **vision**?

Developing Literacy
Word Level Year 5
© A & C Black

Sniff out that homophone

• **Write a homophone for each word. The pictures will help.**

A nose knows a homophone anywhere!

Word	Homophone
son	sun
wring	
prints	
buries	
poll	

Word	Homophone
rows	
thrown	
ate	
plain	
pair	

Word	Homophone
towed	
sale	
sore	
tale	
male	

Now try this!

• **List six other words which have a homophone.**

_____

• **There are two possible homophones for these words. Complete the chart.**

LSCWCh

Word	1st homophone	2nd homophone
there		
pour		
rain		
road		
pear		

Teachers' note The children could make cards from the examples and play a variation of 'Snap'. Link this with sentence-level work on pronouns and the associated confusions, for example, their, there, they're and who's, whose.

Developing Literacy
Word Level Year 5
© A & C Black

Homographs

Homographs are spelled the same but they sound different and have different meanings.

- Write the two different meanings of each word.
- Write a word which rhymes with each homograph.

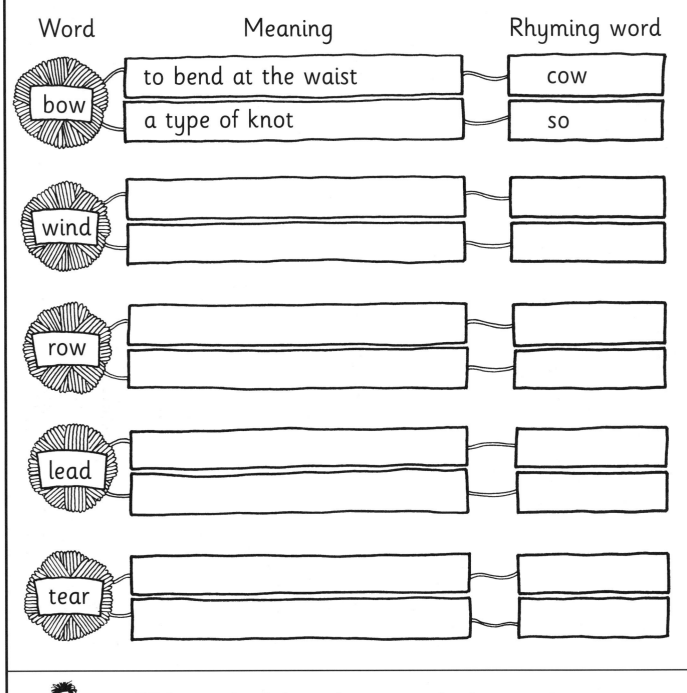

Word	Meaning	Rhyming word
bow	to bend at the waist	cow
	a type of knot	so
wind		
row		
lead		
tear		

Now try this!

- Write each of these homographs in a sentence to show its meaning.

record	record	polish	Polish

Teachers' note Sometimes the difference in meaning between two words which are spelled the same arises because they have different origins. Some of these words with the same pronunciation have two meanings (homonyms), for example, a **row** is a line and to **row** is also to propel a boat.

Developing Literacy
Word Level Year 5
© A & C Black

Spelling riddles

- **Work out the answer to each spelling riddle.**
- **Match the question to the answer.**
- **Write the word.**

What says 'hello' in 'while'?
hi

The (hi) in the middle.

What doesn't sting you although it's at the end of your hand? _____

'Smiles' because there's a mile between the first and the last letter!

How can an @ help a deaf lady? _____

How can you change a word into a dangerous weapon? _____

It makes h(er) h(ear)!

What is the longest six letter word? _____

Put an (s) at the beginning of 'word'!

A (b) on the end of 'thumb'

LSCWCh

- **Which words can you find in** ghost , juice **and** wonderful **?**
- **Write a spelling riddle for each word.**
- **Make up spelling riddles from three other words for a partner to solve**

Now try this!

Teachers' note This is a fun activity which aims to encourage the children to look closely at the sounds which words make and the letters which make up the words.

Developing Literacy
Word Level Year 5
© A & C Black

Remembering spellings

- **Write a mnemonic to help you to remember how to spell these words. You can use the clues in the boxes.**

te | ache | r

Teachers are a pain.
They contain an ache.

eleph | ant

list | ener

temper | ature

govern | ment

a | cross

of | ten

Now try this!

- **Write a mnemonic to help you to remember how to spell** lovely , bought **and** company .
- **How does** Never eat shredded wheat **help you to remember the points of a compass?**

Teachers' note Model an example with the children to explore the idea of words within words, for example, we must **rent** a diffe**rent** house.

**Developing Literacy
Word Level Year 5
© A & C Black**

Plurals rule chart

- **Complete the rules to remind yourself how to change singulars to plurals.**
- **Complete the missing singulars and plurals.**
- **Add two other examples for each rule.**

Use a dictionary.

Rules	Singular	Plural
Most nouns just add $\boxed{s}$.	cat button sock	cats buttons socks
Many nouns ending with a consonant + $\boxed{y}$ change the $\boxed{y}$ to $\boxed{ies}$.	lady	ladies
Nouns ending with a vowel + $\boxed{y}$ _____ _____	day	_____
Many nouns ending with $\boxed{f}$ or $\boxed{fe}$ change this to _____ _____	wolf	_____
Nouns ending with $\boxed{ch}$, $\boxed{sh}$, $\boxed{ss}$ or $\boxed{x}$ add _____ _____	_____	brushes
Nouns ending with a vowel + $\boxed{o}$ add _____	patio	_____
Nouns ending with a consonant + $\boxed{o}$ add _____	_____	volcanoes

Now try this!

- **What groups of plurals are not included in the chart? The word** $\boxed{\text{sheep}}$ **may help.**
- **Write a rule for these plurals and give three other examples.**

Teachers' note This work links closely with sentence-level work but the focus should be on spelling the words and how the rules can help the children to develop independent strategies. It would be helpful to make a large chart for classroom display to which children could add new words.

Negative prefixes

- Choose a 'negative' prefix from the computer screen to make the opposite of each word. Write the new word.

Use a dictionary.

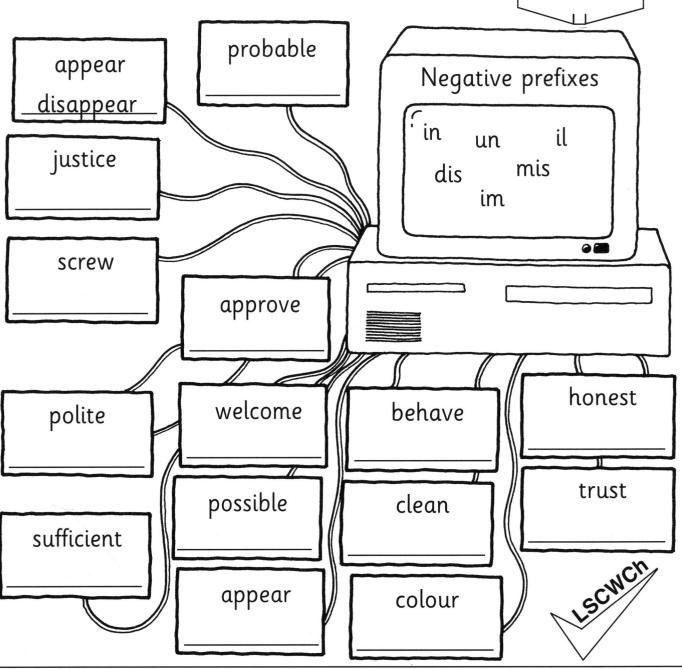

appear
disappear
_____

probable
_____

Negative prefixes

in   un   il
dis   mis
im

justice
_____

screw
_____

approve
_____

polite
_____

welcome
_____

behave
_____

honest
_____

possible
_____

clean
_____

trust
_____

sufficient
_____

appear
_____

colour
_____

LSCWCh

Now try this!

- Does the spelling of the root word change when you add a negative prefix? _____
- Write three other examples of words with a negative prefix. _____
- Write a sentence for each of your examples.

Teachers' note Most children can make negatives using **un** or **dis**; challenge them to find other ways in which words can be made negative. Words should be collected and included on the word wall so that the children can make use of them during writing sessions.

Developing Literacy
Word Level Year 5
© A & C Black

Prefix opposites

- **Circle the prefix in each word.**
- **Write the meaning of the prefix.**
- **Write two other words which have the same prefix.**

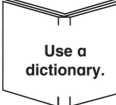

Use a dictionary.

Word	Meaning of prefix	Words with the same prefix
(anti)freeze	against	antiseptic, antibiotic
pre-date		
maximise		
submarine		
inhale		
unicorn		
multicoloured		
exhale		
monocycle		
minimise		
surtax		
post-date		

Now try this!

- **Write the meanings of these two words.**

  | maximise | | minimise |

LSCWCh

- **From your chart, choose two other pairs of words with opposite meanings. Write the words and their meanings.**

Teachers' note The children may be able to deduce from the words the meaning of the prefix. If not, they will find them in a dictionary. Some prefixes have more than one meaning. The children must choose the correct meaning for that word and use that meaning in the new words they write.

Developing Literacy
Word Level Year 5
© A & C Black

Extending words

- **Building words can be like extending a house.**
- **Make new words. Write the words.**

dis-

re-

un-

-ing   -ed

-ment   -s   -d

You may have to change the ending of the root word.

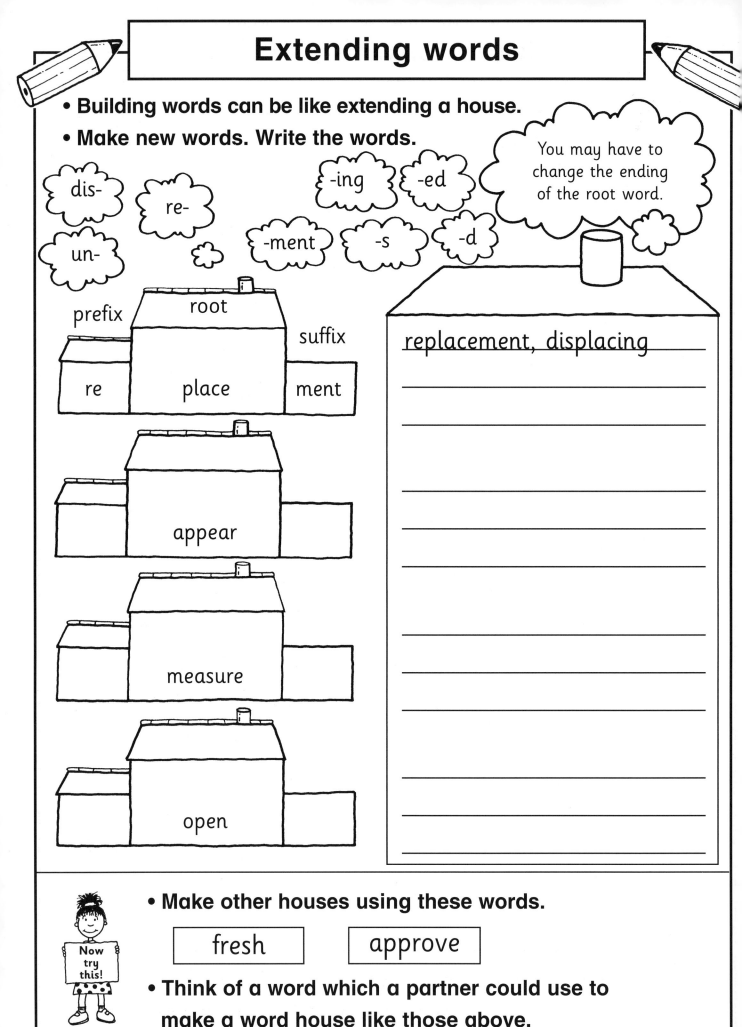

prefix   root   suffix

re   place   ment

appear

measure

open

replacement, displacing

_____

_____

_____

_____

_____

_____

_____

_____

_____

_____

_____

_____

- **Make other houses using these words.**

fresh   approve

- **Think of a word which a partner could use to make a word house like those above.**

Teachers' note This page is investigatory; some children will produce more words than others. Collect a complete list during the plenary session. The idea of 'word houses' could be used for classroom display. The new words then become a resource for shared and guided writing.

Developing Literacy
Word Level Year 5
© A & C Black

Root words fireworks

- Write words which contain the root word around each firework.
- Write in brackets whether you added a prefix (P) or suffix (S).

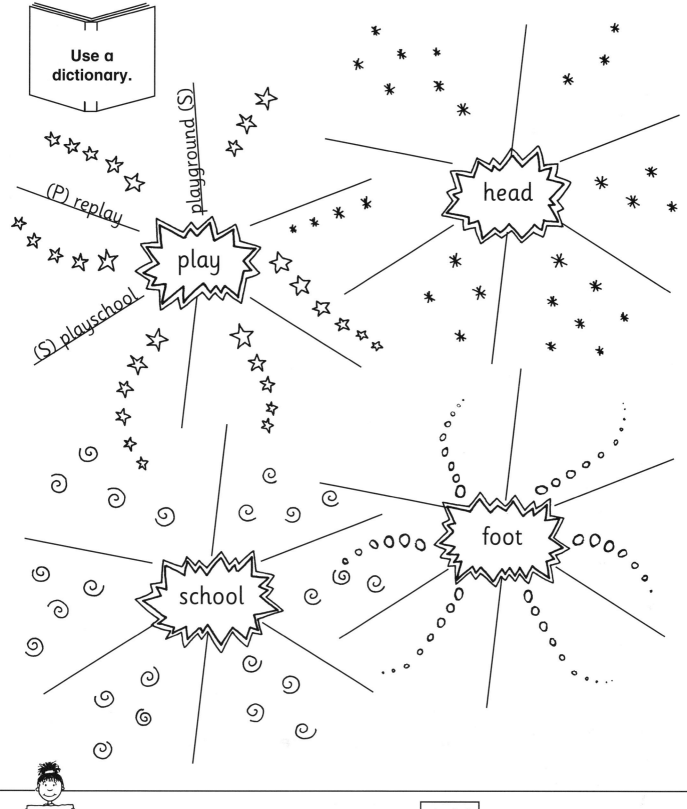

Use a dictionary.

playground (S)

(P) replay

play

(S) playschool

head

foot

school

Now try this!

- Make another firework using child .
- Write eight of the most unusual words in sentences.

Teachers' note Use the information from the sheet for the classroom display. How many different words were found? Which were more frequent, prefixes or suffixes? These language investigations could be developed for the children to carry out at home.

Developing Literacy
Word Level Year 5
© A & C Black

full and all words

Many years ago the way in which people said things was different from today.

Pray tell me, art thou full of cheer?

Yes, I'm cheerful.

- **Write the following in modern English.**
- **Circle any changes in the spelling of the root word.**

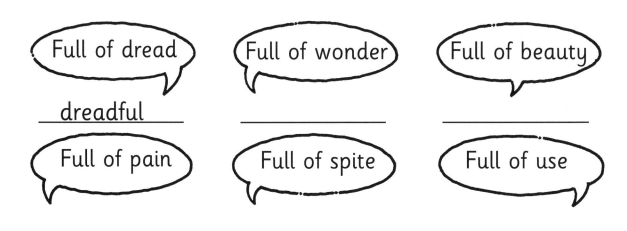

Full of dread

dreadful

Full of wonder

_____

Full of beauty

_____

Full of pain

_____

Full of spite

_____

Full of use

_____

- **How does the spelling of** full **change when it is added to the end of a word?** _____

- **Add** all **to the beginning of each word below.**

ready _____   together _____

most _____   mighty _____

though _____   so _____

- **How does the spelling of** all **change when it is added to the beginning of a word?** _____

Now try this!

- **Write two other examples of** full **words and** all **words.**
- **Use your words in sentences.**

Teachers' note This sheet concentrates on a common spelling error. Work on it should be developed and repeated at appropriate times as well as during the Literacy Hour. Make a large display of the speech bubbles on the sheet which will remind the children of the key words.

Developing Literacy
Word Level Year 5
© A & C Black

Doubling the final consonant

- **Add the endings to the words in the box. Copy and complete the chart with the new words.**

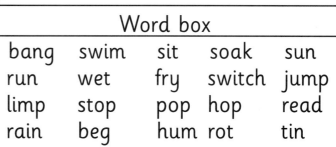

Word box

bang	swim	sit	soak	sun
run	wet	fry	switch	jump
limp	stop	pop	hop	read
rain	beg	hum	rot	tin

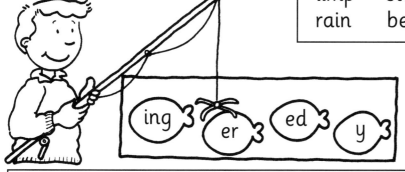

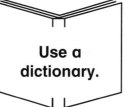

Use a dictionary.

New words

ing	er	ed	y
banging swimming	swimmer	banged	runny

Now try this!

- **Circle all the new words which doubled their final letters.**
- **Look at the circled words and answer the questions.**
  - ★ How many syllables are in these words?_____
  - ★ Is the final letter in the original word a vowel or a consonant?_____
  - ★ Is the letter before the last letter a vowel or a consonant? _____
- **Would the answers be the same with words where the letters did not double? _____**
- **Write a rule to explain when you should double the final consonant before adding a suffix.**

Teachers' note The rule is that in a single-syllable word where a vowel precedes a final consonant, the final consonant will double when endings are added, for example, stop - stopped - stopping, hop - hopped. Discuss examples such as hope - hoped and why they are different.

Soft and hard consonants

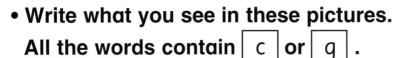

• **Write what you see in these pictures.**

 All the words contain [c] **or** [g] .

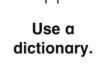
Use a dictionary.

  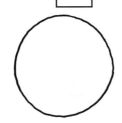 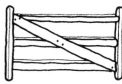

 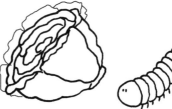  

• **Write these words on the correct pages below.**

Soft [c]	Hard [c]	Soft [g]	Hard [g]
cycle			

Now try this!

• **Which letters come after a soft** [c] **or a soft** [g] **?** _____

• **Which letters come after a hard** [c] **or a hard** [g] **?** _____

• **Add two other examples to each page of hard and**

 soft [c] **and** [g] .

32

Teachers' note Soft **c** and **g** sounds are often followed by **e**, **i** or **y**. Hard **c** and **g** sounds are often followed by **a**, **u**, **o** or consonants, for example, **cycle**, **gum**, **comb**. Poetry can be linked with consonant sounds, for example, hard sounds are aggressive, soft sounds are gentle.

Developing Literacy
Word Level Year 5
© A & C Black

Same letters, different sound

- Write three words on the roundabouts which have the same second sound as the word on the roof.
- Write a word below which uses the same letters making a different sound.

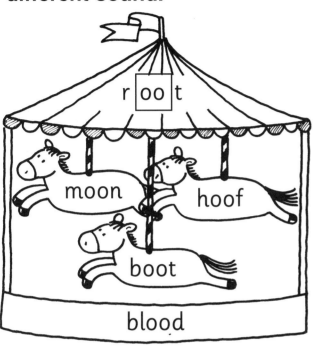

r o͟o t

moon   hoof

boot

blood

m e͟a t

f i͟e ld

th o͟u͟g͟h t

Now try this!

- Draw a word roundabout for these sounds.

a͟i as in r a͟i n

o͟u as in sh o͟u t

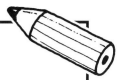

Teachers' note Link with earlier work on the appropriate phonemes with different spellings and with homophones. The idea of roundabouts could be used for classroom collection and display of such words.

Developing Literacy
Word Level Year 5
© A & C Black

Spelling pronouns

- **Work with a partner. Take turns.**
- **Choose a card. Read the word. Say the word in a sentence.**
- **Your partner writes the sentence.**
- **If your partner spells the word wrongly, correct it.**
- **Explain which words are possessive pronouns and why.**

who	hers	you	it's
who's	its	my	theirs
your	yours	whose	they're
there	you're	mine	ours

Now try this!

- **Explain the difference between these words.**

their, there, they're	whose, who's

- **Explain why some of the words above have an apostrophe and some do not.**

Teachers' note The focus of the sheet is spelling, not necessarily grammar, although the children must understand the part of speech before they can identify the correct spelling. There is confusion between the forms of there/their/they're; mine, whose, its, etc.

**Developing Literacy
Word Level Year 5
© A & C Black**

This is the end!

- **Complete these names.**

| What do you call a dog from Alsace? | What is the name of a spotted dog from Dalmatia? | What do we call a person from Venice? | If you are from Egypt, what are you called? |

_____ _____ _____ _____

- **Which word ending do they all have?** _____

- **Change these verbs to nouns.**

- **Which ending do you add to them?**

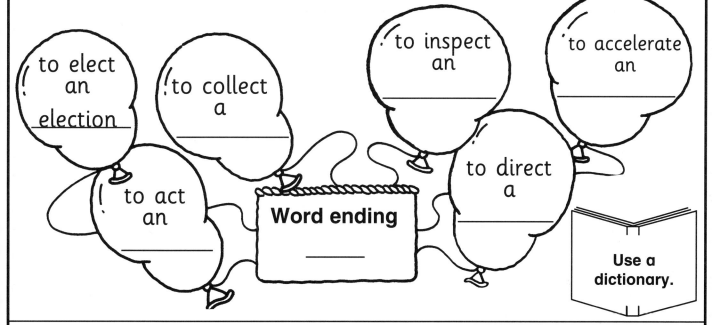

to elect an election

to collect a _____

to inspect an _____

to accelerate an _____

to act an _____

Word ending _____

to direct a _____

Use a dictionary.

Now try this!

- **Write the names of these jobs. They both have the same ending.**

A person who plays music is called a _____ .

A person who works in politics is called a _____ .

- **Write another job name with the same ending.** _____

Teachers' note Take the opportunity to investigate other letter combinations which make the **shun** sound. Link with sentence-level work on the transition between different parts of speech and the spelling issues which arise.

Developing Literacy
Word Level Year 5
© A & C Black

Long word spelling

- Join a syllable from each group to make a word.
- Write the word on the notepad.
- Divide the word into syllables.

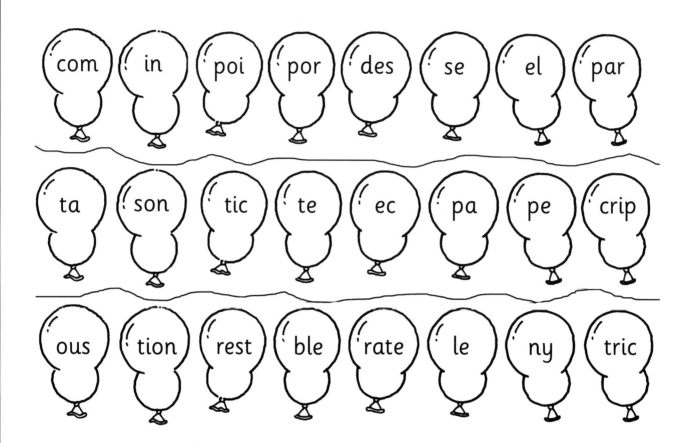

com | in | poi | por | des | se | el | par

ta | son | tic | te | ec | pa | pe | crip

ous | tion | rest | ble | rate | le | ny | tric

se/pa/rate _____   _____   _____

_____   _____   _____

_____   _____

- **Check the meanings in a dictionary.**

Now try this!

- **In the words you have made, circle the vowels which are often missed out by mistake.**
- **Think of mnemonics to help you to remember how to spell these words and not leave out the tricky vowels.**

Teachers' note Another useful way to help the children to recognise the unstressed vowel in these polysyllabic words is to ask them to draw the shapes of the words and notice where the vowels come. The use of a multi-sensory approach helps with some children.

Developing Literacy
Word Level Year 5
© A & C Black

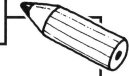

Silent $\boxed{e}$

- **Read the word. Add $\boxed{e}$. Write the new word.**
- **Read the new word.**

mat
fat
gap
hat
mad
rat
at
kit
rip
pip
fin
win
slim
cub

Think!
How do the
new words
sound different ?

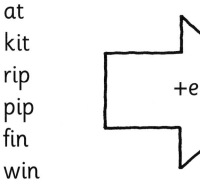

+e

mate

- **Complete the rule.**

Rule

The silent $\boxed{e}$ makes the

vowel sound —————

—————————————

—————————————

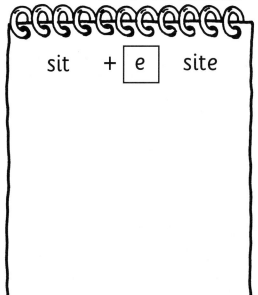

sit   + $\boxed{e}$ site

- **Write some other examples on the notepad which prove your rule.**

Now
try
this!

- **Use five pairs of words from your examples in sentences, for example,** I hate the hat on that cat.

Teachers' note This is a simple but often overlooked principle and many spelling rules depend upon children's ability able to recognise a long or a short vowel. It is also interesting for children to realise how, by adding just one letter, they can completely change the sound and the meaning of a word.

Developing Literacy
Word Level Year 5
© A & C Black

ly

Adverbs describe verbs. They mostly end in $\boxed{ly}$.

• **Free the words from their prison. Write the words in the chart.**

Change them into adverbs. Copy and complete the chart.

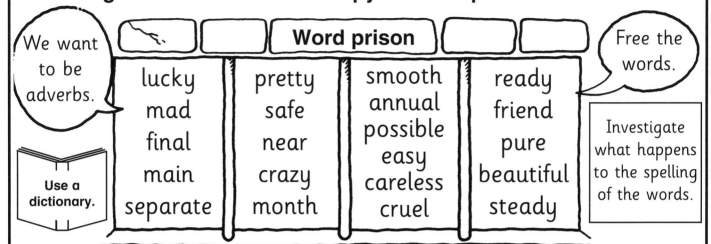

We want to be adverbs.

Use a dictionary.

Word prison

lucky	pretty	smooth	ready
mad	safe	annual	friend
final	near	possible	pure
main	crazy	easy	beautiful
separate	month	careless	steady
		cruel	

Free the words.

Investigate what happens to the spelling of the words.

Word	Adverb	Any changes in spelling
lucky	luckily	y changes to i before ly.

Now try this!

• **Write a rule for adding $\boxed{ly}$ when the word ends in $\boxed{y}$.**

• **List the adverbs you can use after spoke,**

for example, She spoke quietly.

Teachers' note Link this activity with sentence-level work on adverbs. It is important for the children to realise that not all adverbs end with **ly**; examples of these should be listed, for example, fast. It is helpful to discuss the idea of comparatives and superlatives at this stage and to show how they are spelled.

Developing Literacy
Word Level Year 5
© A & C Black

Love |ly| words

Most adverbs are formed by adding |ly|.

- Add |ly| to these words. Write the words.
- Circle the |ly| and the letter which comes before.

Use a dictionary.

love   lov(ely)

stupid   _____

nice   _____   especial   _____

thankful   _____   financial   _____

general   _____   final   _____

immediate   _____   grateful   _____

- Add |ly| to these words.

simple   _____   single   _____

terrible   _____   probable   _____

possible   _____

miserable   _____

- What happens when you add |ly| to words ending with |le| ?

_____

_____

_____   LSCWCh ✓

Now try this!

- Make adverbs from these words and use them in sentences.

| happy | sad | hopeful | miserable |

Teachers' note Some adverbs have the same form as adjectives, for example, fast, hard, long. Remind the children that not all words ending in **ly** are adverbs, for example, ugly and holy. If a word ends with **le**, the **le** is dropped before adding **ly**.

Developing Literacy
Word Level Year 5
© A & C Black

i before e

i before e except after c , whenever it rhymes with me .

- **Read the words on the bricks.**
- **Check that you understand the rule.**
- **Write each word on the correct wall.**

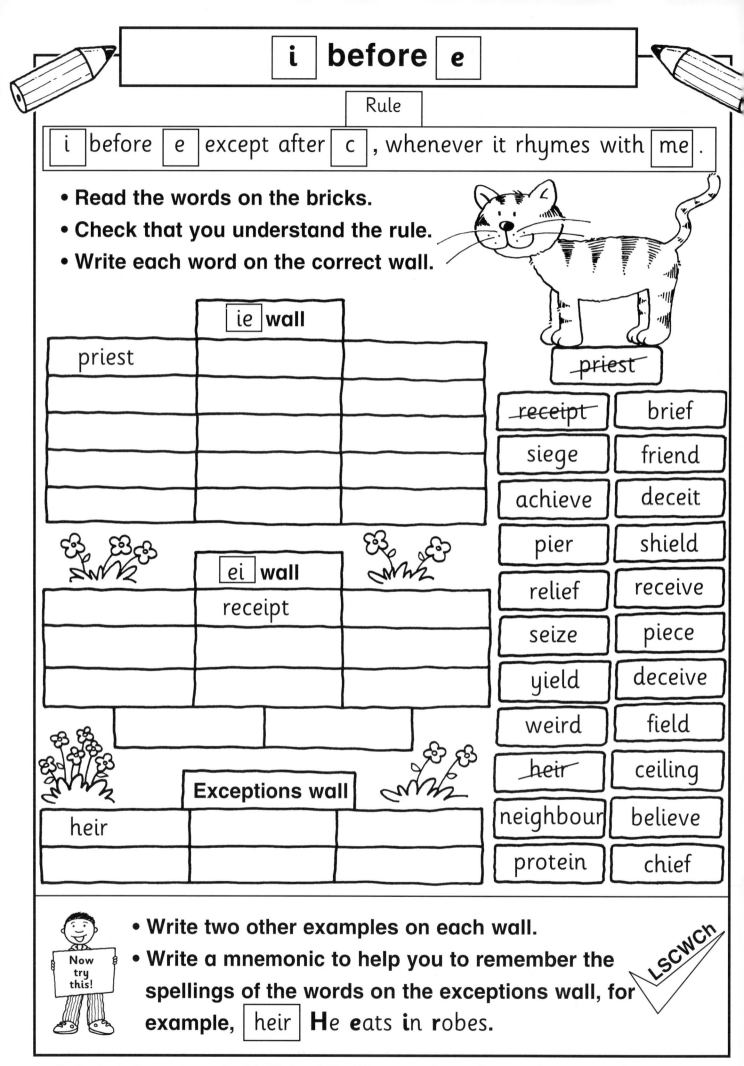

ie wall

priest		

ei wall

	receipt	

Exceptions wall

heir		

priest

receipt	brief
siege	friend
achieve	deceit
pier	shield
relief	receive
seize	piece
yield	deceive
weird	field
heir	ceiling
neighbour	believe
protein	chief

Now try this!

- **Write two other examples on each wall.**
- **Write a mnemonic to help you to remember the spellings of the words on the exceptions wall, for example,** heir **H**e **e**ats **i**n **r**obes.

LSCWCh

Teachers' note Create a class word wall for 'i before e'. The children can continue to add new words as they find them.

Developing Literacy Word Level Year 5 © A & C Black

Words ending in y

- How many words can you make by adding the suffixes on the wire to the words in the cable cars?
You may have to remove some letters before adding the suffix.

| ful | ed | es | est | ly | ness | able |

Verbs
carry   reply
worry   bully
supply   dry
envy   rely
marry   hurry

Nouns
baby   ruby

mercy   lady

body

Adjectives
happy   easy

lazy   beauty

steady

carried

Use a dictionary.

- What happens to y when you add the suffix?

LSCWCh

Now try this!

- Add ing to the first five verbs. Write the new words.

- Adding ing is different from adding the other suffixes. How?

Teachers' note Revise plurals ending in **y** and the rule 'y changes to i except if there is a vowel before it'. Check that the children understand the effect of adding phonemes at the end, that is, words ending in **e** drop the **e** when adding **ing**, otherwise **ei** together would make an **ee** sound.

Developing Literacy
Word Level Year 5
© A & C Black

41

Transforming words

When words change from one part of speech to another their endings change.

• Complete the chart.

Use a dictionary.

Adjective	Noun	Changes in spelling
young	youth	– ng before +th
beautiful		
loyal		
long		
wide		
warm		
deep		
strong		
lonely		
friendly		
good		

LSCWCh

Now try this!

• Change these nouns to verbs. Complete the chart.

Noun	Verb	Changes in spelling
a knee	to kneel	add l to end of word
a threat		
a spark		
an action		

Teachers' note Link this activity with sentence-level work on transforming from one part of speech to another. Once the children have changed the words on the sheet, give them a word, ask which part of speech it is and ask them to change it back again.

Developing Literacy
Word Level Year 5
© A & C Black

New word endings

The meaning of words can be changed by adding new endings.

• Read the word. Write a sentence using the word.

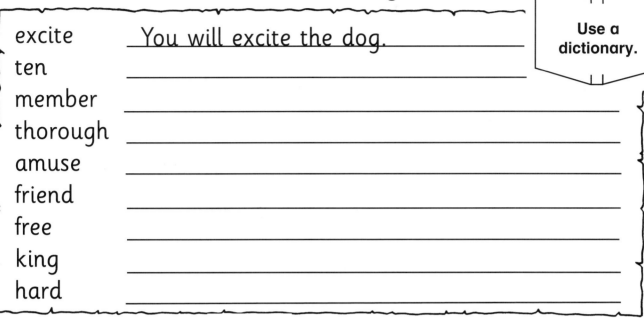

excite	You will excite the dog.
ten	
member	
thorough	
amuse	
friend	
free	
king	
hard	

Use a dictionary.

• Add a word ending from the wall. Complete the chart.

• List the new meanings.

• Explain how the meanings of the words have changed.

_____

_____

Word endings

th	ship	ment
	ness	dom

Word	New word
excite	excitement
ten	
member	
thorough	
amuse	
friend	
free	
king	
hard	

Now try this!

• **Write another ending which will change these words.** _____
• **Use your ending to make six new words.**
• **Write them in sentences.**

Teachers' note Use this activity in connection with sentence-level work (changing into adjectives, and nouns, often abstract nouns).

**Developing Literacy
Word Level Year 5
© A & C Black**

Synonyms for describing faces

- **Choose someone in your class.**
- **Describe each feature in the diagram.**
- **Complete the chart with at least two synonyms to describe each feature.**

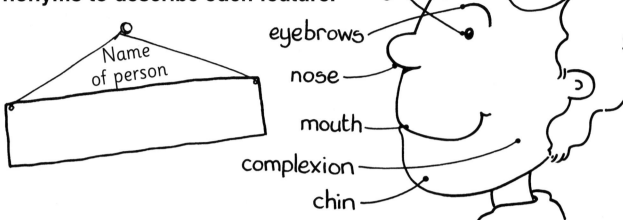

Name of person

forehead

hair

eyes

eyebrows

nose

mouth

complexion

chin

Feature	Shape	Size	Colour	Texture	Other words
forehead	rounded curved	large enormous	pale white		

Now try this!

- **Use the information in the chart to write a description of the person.**
- **Tick the words you used in your chart. Why did you choose them?** _____

Teachers' note Use the sheets as the basis for writing 'Missing' police reports on individual children. When they are read aloud, are the descriptions good enough to enable the group to guess who it is? Discuss which are the best words to use and the fine distinctions in meaning between synonyms.

Developing Literacy
Word Level Year 5
© A & C Black

Antonym 'Snap'

Antonyms are opposites.

- **Work with a partner. Complete the antonyms.**
- **Cut out the cards. Play 'Snap'.**

Use a dictionary.

Word	Antonym	Word	Antonym
stale	fresh	healthy	
rude		clean	
bitter		loose	
love		before	
truth		often	
deep		wealth	
rough		careless	
false		straight	
hollow		ancient	
warm		clear	
right		absent	
cheap		valuable	
huge		coarse	

Teachers' note Photocopy or glue this sheet on to card. The children play 'Snap' and may collect the cards only after explaining why the words are opposites. They should be encouraged to add their own pairs of antonyms to extend the game. The cards could also be displayed as bricks on a word wall.

**Developing Literacy
Word Level Year 5
© A & C Black**

Cracking proverbs

Proverbs never mean exactly what they say.

They use an idea to teach us something.

- Join the two halves of the proverbs.
- Write the proverbs.

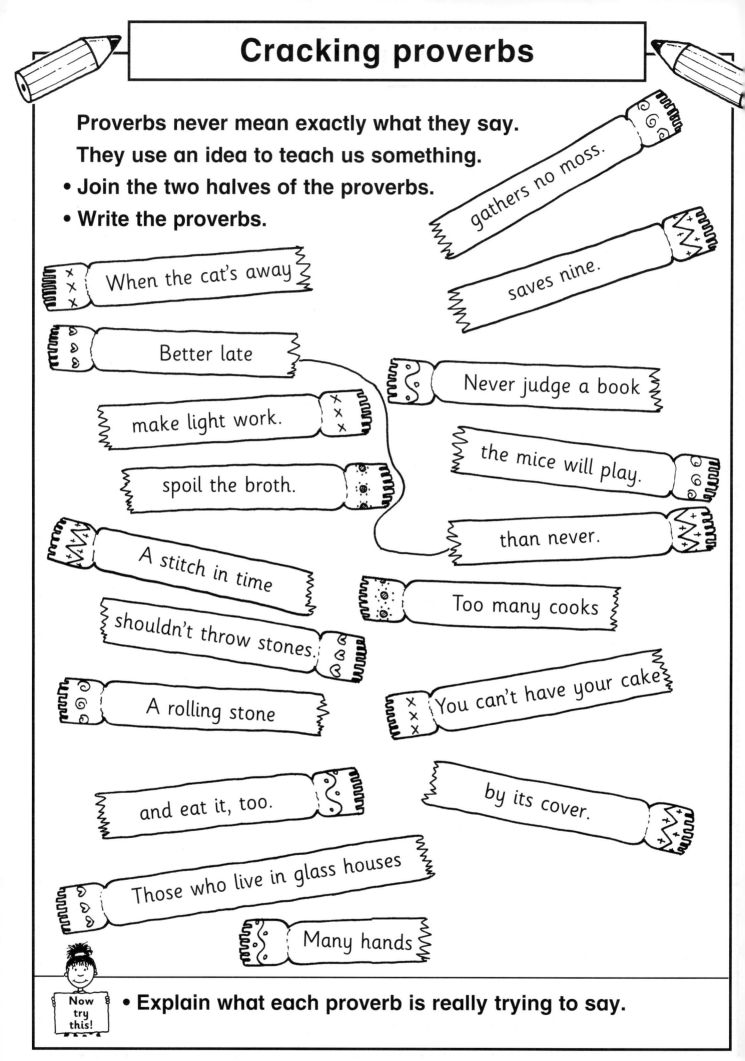

gathers no moss.

saves nine.

When the cat's away

Better late

Never judge a book

make light work.

the mice will play.

spoil the broth.

than never.

A stitch in time

Too many cooks

shouldn't throw stones.

A rolling stone

You can't have your cake

and eat it, too.

by its cover.

Those who live in glass houses

Many hands

Now try this!

- **Explain what each proverb is really trying to say.**

Teachers' note The children should be aware of proverbs as a genre, just as they should be aware of fables and myths. However, make it clear, during directed writing sessions, that over-use of proverbs will make their writing vague and cliché-ridden.

**Developing Literacy
Word Level Year 5
© A & C Black**

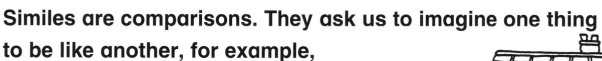

Similes

Similes are comparisons. They ask us to imagine one thing
to be like another, for example,

The windows of the house are  like eyes.

Similes use like or as .

- **Write the similes shown in these pictures.**

As thin as a rake.

  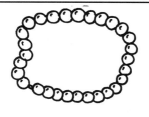

  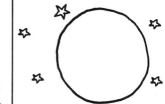 

- **Complete these to make your own similes:**
  He climbed like a _____ .
  Berries as red as _____ .
  Snow as white as _____ .
- **Write five other similes.**

Teachers' note There are no correct answers. The idea is to be as imaginative as possible, for example, 'as white as my mum's sheets when they have been washed three times' is better than 'as white as snow'. Children could use them as a basis for list poems, for example, As red as ..., etc.

**Developing Literacy
Word Level Year 5
© A & C Black**

47

Using metaphors

- **Change these metaphorical expressions into similes to explain what they mean.**

Nurses are the backbone of our hospitals.

Nurses are like backbones because they provide support. You cannot do without them.

The moon's a yellow balloon in the sky.

_____
_____
_____

The car flew down the motorway.

_____
_____
_____

The sea is a mirror for the sunset.

_____
_____
_____

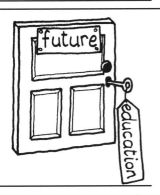

Education is your key to the future.

_____
_____
_____

Her words are poison.

_____
_____
_____

Now try this!

- **Write five other metaphorical expressions you use, for example,** It's raining cats and dogs!
- **Explain the comparisons you are using.**

Teachers' note Metaphors are difficult to explain. Start from similes and remind the children that metaphors are statements, probably impossible in themselves. That is why it is useful to draw cartoons to illustrate the comparisons.

Developing Literacy
Word Level Year 5
© A & C Black

Animal onomatopoeia

Onomatopoeic words are sound words. The words make the sound you are describing, for example, woof, for a dog's bark.

- The sound box contains animal sounds. Write the sounds in the correct animal. Some animals have more than one word.

Sound box

howl, roar, yelp, growl, snarl, grunt, squeak, neigh, purr, bleat, moo, croak, screech, caw, gobble, quack, cluck, cheep, chirp, twitter, hum, buzz, hiss, whinny.

purr

Now try this!

- List six onomatopoeic words, not to do with animals, for example, crack.
- Use them in sentences.

LSCWCh

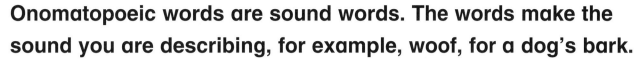

Teachers' note This is a simple introduction to onomatopoeia. Examine how the letter combinations in the words make the sounds and distinguish between hard and soft sounds, for example, **ck** and **sh**.

Developing Literacy
Word Level Year 5
© A & C Black

Sound poems

Splat! Clash! Pop! Sploosh!

• **Write sound poems by completing the spaces.**

I love music.
The __boom__ of __drums__ .
The _____ of _____ .
The _____ of _____ .
The _____ of _____ .
The _____ of _____ .
I like music.

I love sport.
The __thud__ of __a football__ .
The _____ of _____ .
The _____ of _____ .
The _____ of _____ .
I like sport.

Now try this!

• **Write another 'I love ...' sound poem.**
• **Think about how you could best perform it.**

Teachers' note This is a creative development of easier work on onomatopoeia. Discuss with the children the use of the words as verbs, for example, crash, crashed, crashing. What happens with words such as snap? The outlines could be used as templates for display or book making.

Developing Literacy
Word Level Year 5
© A & C Black

Foreign phrases

Here are some well-known words and phrases which come from other languages.

* Complete the fact files.

Use a dictionary.

encore
Original language: _French_

Meaning: _____

_____

Used in a sentence: _____

_____

_____

vice versa
Original language: _____

Meaning: _____

_____

Used in a sentence: _____

_____

_____

post-mortem
Original language: _____

Meaning: _____

_____

Used in a sentence: _____

_____

_____

hors d'oeuvres
Original language: _____

Meaning: _____

_____

Used in a sentence: _____

_____

_____

bon voyage
Original language: _____

Meaning: _____

_____

Used in a sentence: _____

_____

_____

fiancé
Original language: _____

Meaning: _____

_____

Used in a sentence: _____

_____

_____

Now try this!

* Write a fact file for these, including what the abbreviations stand for. | a.m. | | p.m. | | A.D.
* Write three other words or phrases we use in English which come from other languages.
* Write a fact file for each one.

Teachers' note French and Latin have had considerable influence on English. Make lists of other French and Latin words the children can find. Discuss how French pronunciation has changed the spelling of words, for example, garage, ballet.

World English

- **Write the words which come from India or Italy in the country outline.**
- **List words which come from other countries, with the country from which they come, in the box below.**

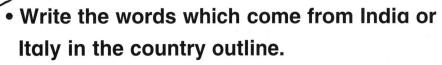

Use a dictionary.

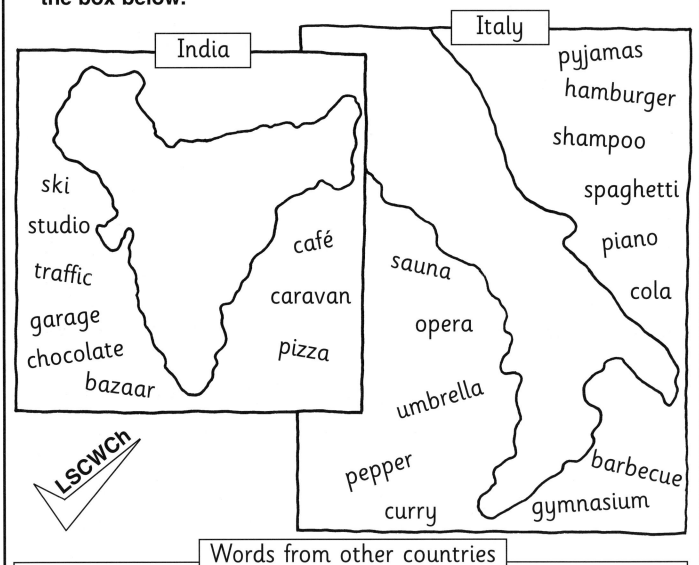

India

Italy

pyjamas
hamburger
shampoo
spaghetti
piano
cola

ski
studio
traffic
garage
chocolate
bazaar

café
caravan
pizza

sauna
opera

umbrella

pepper
curry

barbecue
gymnasium

LSCWCh

Words from other countries

hamburger – Germany

Now try this!

- **List more words which come from the other countries.**
- **Write six of the words in sentences.**

Teachers' note* Much work on word derivation can be linked in with other subject areas. Many Indian words came to Britain during Victorian times because of British involvement in India. English is not a static language and is ever-changing (see Computer words, page 55).

Developing Literacy
Word Level Year 5
© A & C Black

American accents and words

- **Read these two poems and you will be imitating the accent of the Bronx area of New York.**
- **Write the poems in standard English.**
- **Underline in red the words which now have a different spelling.**

Work in pairs.

Toity poiple boids
Sitt'n on der coib
A' choipin and a' boipin
An' eat'n doity woims.

Spring in New York
Der spring is sprung
Der grass is riz
I wonder where dem boidies is?
Der liddle boids is on der wing.
Ain't dat absoid?
Der liddle wings is on der boid!

- **Write the words we would use instead of these American words:**

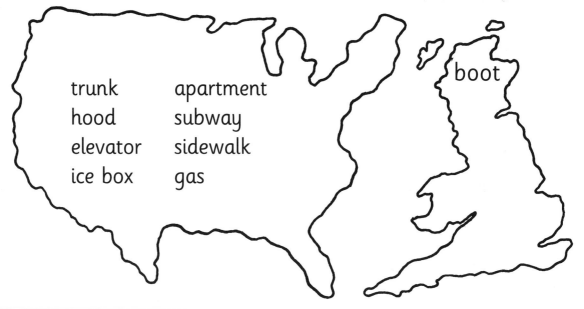

trunk   apartment
hood   subway
elevator   sidewalk
ice box   gas

boot

Now try this!

- **Work with a partner. List six words which are pronounced differently in America.**

Teachers' note* This is a fun way to show that American is different from standard English, even though both are English. It is important to stress that standard English often pronounces words in a different way, for example, lieutenant.

Developing Literacy
Word Level Year 5
© A & C Black

A cockney poem

- **Read this poem and you will be imitating a cockney accent.**
- **Write it out in the box below, using standard English.**
- **Underline in red the cockney words which now have a different spelling.**

Work in pairs.

A muvver was barfin' 'er biby one night,
The youngest of ten and a tiny young mite;
The muvver was pore, an' the biby was fin,
Only a skellington covered wiv skin.
The muvver turned rahnd for the soap orf the rack,
The biby was gorn, and in anguish she cried,
'Oh, where is my biby?' – The angels replied:
'Your biby 'as fell dahn the plug-'ole,
Your biby 'as gorn dahn the plug;
The pore lickle fing was so skinny an' fin,
'E oughter bin barfed in a jug.'

_____
_____
_____
_____
_____
_____
_____
_____
_____
_____
_____

Now try this!

- **Compare your new version with a friend's.**
  Have you spelled the standard English version correctly?
- **Practise a performance of the poem.**

Teachers' note The point of dealing with standard English is to discuss the appropriateness of language in certain situations. It is important to stress that there is nothing 'wrong' with local dialect or with non-standard English. The children should be thinking about appropriate language for different audiences.

Developing Literacy
Word Level Year 5
© A & C Black

Computer words

Words to do with computers are new or have had to change their meaning.

• Unscramble the words and label the computer.

tiomron	yokabred	rripent	DC ORM
rahd vierd	medom	pplofy kisd	seoum

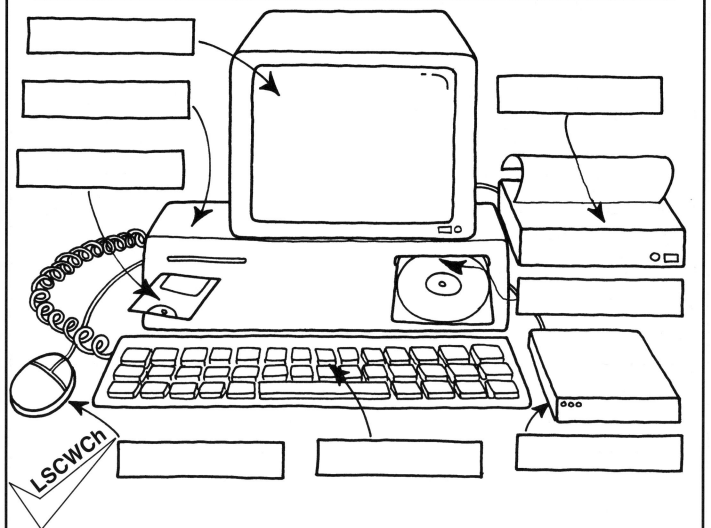

LSCWCh

The Internet is even more recent.

• **Write the meaning of these words and phrases.**

1. world-wide web _____

2. home pages _____

3. browser _____

4. e-mail _____

5. surf the net _____

Teachers' note* The children should be able to identify the parts of the computer at home or in the classroom and discuss how new words come about. An interesting development is the new language developing over the Internet and how people communicate in writing via e-mail.

Developing Literacy
Word Level Year 5
© A & C Black

55

Maths words

• **Complete the chart.**

Object	Name of object	Adjective	Changes in spelling
◯	a c i r c l e	circular	
▢	a s _ _ _ _ _ _		
△	a t _ _ _ _ _ _ _ _		
▭	a r _ _ _ _ _ _ _ _		
◇	a p _ _ _ _ _ _		
●	a sp _ _ _ _ _		
⬛	a c _ _ _ _		
cylinder	a c _ _ _ _ _ _ _ _		
cone	a c _ _ _ _		
angle	an an _ _ _ _		

• **Complete the sentences with a shape adjective from above.**

A window is _____ .

A die is _____ .

A mug is _____ .

A football is _____ .

Use a dictionary.

LSCWCh

Now try this!

• **Write a sentence about the shape of eight other objects.**

• **What pattern can you see in the endings of the adjectives?** _____

_____

Teachers' note This sheet can be used as a development of work from sentence-level, changing one part of speech to another and noticing the impact of this on spelling. This word bank is from maths. Develop others from science, in which difficult words abound, for example, salt, salty, saline.

Developing Literacy
Word Level Year 5
© A & C Black

56

'A lot of' words

Special words exist to describe 'a lot of' something.

- **Find them in the wordsearch.**

A lot of: cattle passages new houses applause
snow people who want to cause trouble
ships people who want to worship
money

h	s	x	b	a	r	w	q	e	x	p	t
e	d	s	v	b	l	i	z	z	a	r	d
r	t	f	o	r	t	u	n	e	o	f	y
d	u	z	i	b	f	m	o	b	a	n	z
v	x	c	w	b	l	f	g	a	e	y	m
c	o	n	g	r	e	g	a	t	i	o	n
r	c	g	g	x	e	w	e	q	y	d	l
h	c	l	j	b	t	u	m	l	j	n	v
q	t	k	k	s	f	l	g	p	z	a	k
e	s	t	a	t	e	r	l	i	h	o	q
p	m	p	o	v	a	t	i	o	n	i	j
n	l	a	b	y	r	i	n	t	h	a	o

- **Copy and complete this chart using the words from the wordsearch.**
- **Add five other examples.**

A lot of ...	is called a ...
cattle	herd

Teachers' note* Link this with work in shared and guided writing. It is important that the children become more accurate in their use of language and are challenged with difficult words, as in this puzzle. Help them by supplying some of the letters in the words to make them more easy to find in reference sources.

Developing Literacy
Word Level Year 5
© A & C Black

'Get' new words

There is always a better word for 'get'.

- **Read the clues. Complete the puzzle.**
- **Write the words below and learn them, including their meanings.**

Improve your English. Avoid using 'get'.

Across

3. To get on a horse (5).

5. To get smaller (8).

6. To get better at something (7).

7. To get better from an illness (7).

10. To get richer (7).

Down

1. To get softer in the heat (4).

2. To get started (5).

4. To get in the way (8).

8. To get on a ship (6).

9. To get bigger (4).

1.

2.

3. 4.

5. d i

6. i m

7.   8. e r

9.

10. p r   r

k

Now try this!

- **Use these words in sentences.**
- **Find three other examples of 'get' words.**
  Use a thesaurus to find better words.

Teachers' note* Link this with work in shared and guided writing. It is important that the children become more accurate in their use of language and are challenged with difficult words, as in this puzzle. You can supply some letters in the words to make them easier to find in reference sources.

Developing Literacy
Word Level Year 5
© A & C Black

Secret code

- Cut out the alphabet strip and the code strip.
- Mark a cross on the code strip against a letter of your choice.
  Match the two crosses.
- Write a message in code for your partner to solve.
  Give them your name in code as a clue.

a	b	c	d	e	f	g

a	b	c	d	e	f	g	h	i	j	k

face = jegi

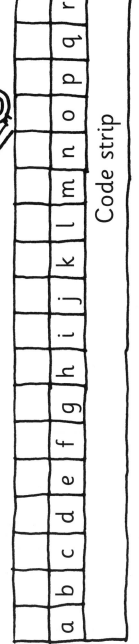

Alphabet strip

a	b	c	d	e	f	g	h	i	j	k	l	m	n	o	p	q	r	s	t	u	v	w	x	y	z

Code strip

a	b	c	d	e	f	g	h	i	j	k	l	m	n	o	p	q	r	s	t	u	v	w	x	y	z

- Use a different code to write a message to
  direct a partner to some treasure.
- Give it to your partner to solve. If necessary,
  give your name as a clue.

Now try this!

Developing Literacy
Word Level Year 5
© A & C Black

Teachers' note Children need to note where they start from each time to inform their partner. Glue another strip on the end of the code strip to ensure that all letters of the alphabet are included. Use words from the medium frequency list for the children to put into code and to decode for other groups. Develop into other work using codes, thus developing alphabet skills and skills in structuring words.

Which dictionary quartile?

- **It is easier to find your way around a dictionary if you think of it in four sections (called quartiles).**
- **Write the words below in the correct quartile. Put them in alphabetical order.**

A-D

~~apologise~~

apologise

liquorice

discourage

republic

E-L

weevil

uneven

lichen

occasional

S-Z

M-R

A-D   E-L

shingle

welfare

unison

resemble

horizontal

shoal

navigate

ocean

freight

M-R

fragment

S-Z

hoarding

appear

backache

diminish

national

banquet

LSCWCh

- **Find the meanings of the words.**
- **Write eight of the most unusual words in sentences.**

Now try this!

Teachers' note The division into these quartiles is traditional. Challenge the children to think of a mnemonic to remember this division. When they have learned the quartiles, they will find their way around a dictionary more quickly. Make up speed games to challenge them to find words.

Developing Literacy
Word Level Year 5
© A & C Black

Alphabetical order

- **Write the words below in the correct sections of the balloon.**
- **Put them in alphabetical order.**

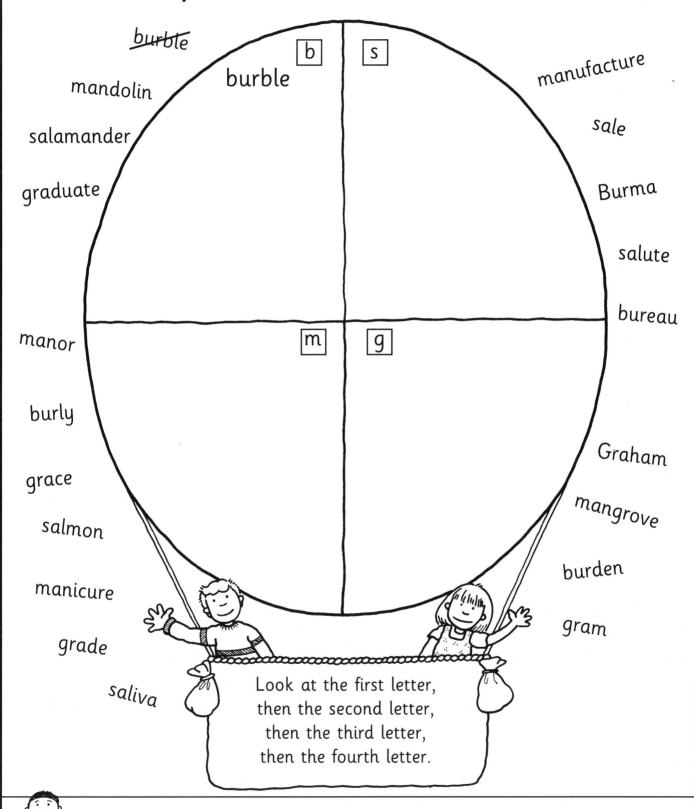

burble

mandolin

salamander

graduate

manor

burly

grace

salmon

manicure

grade

saliva

burble

b   s

m   g

manufacture

sale

Burma

salute

bureau

Graham

mangrove

burden

gram

Look at the first letter,
then the second letter,
then the third letter,
then the fourth letter.

- **Find the meanings of the words in a dictionary.**
- **Write eight of the most unusual words in sentences.**

Now
try
this!

Teachers' note Once the children show confidence at this level of alphabetical order they should then be challenged with alphabetical order to the fifth letter. Link this to other dictionary work (page 60), so that the children become more confident when using reference sources.

**Developing Literacy
Word Level Year 5
© A & C Black**

Meanings game

- **Read the word. Guess the meaning of the word from what you know. Put a cross in the box.**

Work with a partner.

- **Explain your choice. Check the meaning in a dictionary.**

Word: artisan	Possible meaning	Guess x Check ✓
Explanation	a) an artichoke	
	b) an exhibition	
	c) a craftsperson	

Word: colony	Possible meaning	Guess x Check ✓
Explanation	a) to colour in	
	b) a land governed by another nation	
	c) a punctuation mark	

Word: legislation	Possible meaning	Guess x Check ✓
Explanation	a) to draw lines	
	b) laws	
	c) to be late for school	

Word: philanthropist	Possible meaning	Guess x Check ✓
Explanation	a) someone who dispenses medicines at the chemist	
	b) someone who gives generously to help other people	
	c) a sweet Greek pastry	

Teachers' note The game is based on 'Call my Bluff'. Words associated with Victorians have been used here. Difficult words from any subject can be used. A blank set of cards is provided on page 63. The children should use what they know about the words before looking in a dictionary.

Developing Literacy
Word Level Year 5
© A & C Black

Blank meanings cards

Word:	Possible meaning	Guess x Check ✓
Explanation	a)	
	b)	
	c)	

Word:	Possible meaning	Guess x Check ✓
Explanation	a)	
	b)	
	c)	

Word:	Possible meaning	Guess x Check ✓
Explanation	a)	
	b)	
	c)	

Word:	Possible meaning	Guess x Check ✓
Explanation	a)	
	b)	
	c)	

Teachers' note This game is based on 'Call my Bluff' (page 62). Difficult words from any subject area can be used. The children could be given cards bearing only the words. They insert the meaning and two other amusing definitions. One child challenges another by reading the alternatives.

Developing Literacy
Word Level Year 5
© A & C Black

My own dictionary

Name: _____   **Class:** _____

Guide Word:

Word	Meaning

Guide word:

Word	Meaning

Have I used a dictionary to check my spelling?

Do I understand the abbreviations?

Examples:

adj = adjective   v = verb

Gk = Greek   OE = Old English

Have I included guide words ?

Are the words in alphabetical order?

Teachers' note This sheet can be used to teach the children how to find their way around a dictionary as well as acting as a checklist and a pro-forma for personal dictionaries/ glossaries in subject areas, for example geography or science. The children need to learn to use the guide words at the top of dictionary pages to avoid looking through the

Developing Literacy
Word Level Year 5